Glimpses...
NOW I CAN SEE

ELIZABETH A ROBERTS

SWEETSPIRE LITERATURE
MANAGEMENT

Table of Contents

To Cecilia

-for your life, for your love, for your laughter-

And to those dear friends who read selections,
who listened to me read to them,
who granted concern, patience, and support
as my imaginary book took form,
I offer my simple, yet deeply-felt, Thank You.

Preface

The stories, poems, and essays in this book provide "Glimpses" into a life— my life. Some are uncomfortably disturbing, some touchingly poignant, some delightfully humorous. These reflections, these memories, these observations hold me to a path of insight about events, people, and myself. I can now examine my seventy-years with a sense of clear vision. I did not have that clarity for far too many years. During that time, there was a loss of sight, both literally and figuratively. To share with you the frustrations and fears of some of those days of grayness and blackness is but one purpose of this book. I also want to share with you times of joy, of contentment, of peace, and of hope. It is that last word—hope—which makes us survivors. My desire for you, in reading these glimpses, is not only to sense the distress and pain; but also to sense resilience, achievement, and love. Those three, I graciously offer to you.

Allow me to introduce eyesight to you—my eyesight. Telling about my vision seems an appropriate way to begin glimpses into my life— glimpses in many forms. The following introduction tells about my eyesight, the literal loss and restoration of it during two lengthy periods of time. I have also gained figurative sight—insight, as I wish to call it—about people and about events and about moments in time that have been part of my world. All these comprise the glimpses I share with you.

Introduction

Words on paper, features of faces, outlines of new, green leaves on oak and maple trees, and colors of exquisite, yellow blossoms of forsythia and jonquils all became blurred, out-of-focus. My first loss of eyesight began during the spring of 1993. I thought I merely needed minor vision improvement with eyeglasses. I was, after all, forty-nine- years-old. More inconvenienced than seriously concerned, I made an appointment with an optometrist who conducted the usual vision test during which I had to choose "number 1 or number 2, number 2 or number 3," in order to determine how far below "E G N U 5" the letters and numbers were crisp and clear. I hated the selection process. It was like taking the SATs, and I never did well on multiple-choice tests. Was "number 3" correct? Was "number 4" wrong? As with the SATs, time allowed only quick decisions. I wanted to mull over my answers.

I did not pass the test with flying colors. Glasses with appropriate lenses were prescribed. Fourteen days later, the glasses arrived. On a sunny day in mid-June, words, faces, leaves, and flowers once again became distinct and vivid. I was pleased with the sensation. All was well in the vision world.

Six weeks later, all was not well. I was back in the doctor's office, taking the multiple-choice test. During the exam, I sensed no hint of concern as another set of lenses was prescribed. Fourteen days later, my vision improved with crisp, precise results.

October came, and once more I sat in the optometrist's chair. Once more, I had to determine if "number 3" was better or worse. Once more, new glasses arrived. I began to wonder, to inquire why my vision kept altering so frequently. No answers were given.

Early November arrived. As before, vision had improved for a brief period. Then, more blurriness. Then, new lenses. The days of clarity appeared and disappeared like passing mile-markers on a road to who knew where. The optometrist did begin to show concern; but, it was a frustrated, angry concern, short-tempered and abrupt during an examination. And, I began to feel guilty, to feel as though I was not doing the "job-of-seeing" properly, that I was not keeping my side of a visual bargain. I left the practice.

My initial mild distress I felt in April and May was long gone. What I now felt was fear. No longer just slowly encroaching, it had arrived with full force. I had to halt my work as a communications professor. A medical leave-of- absence was granted. I could not drive, nor even walk without grasping an object for stability. My dear friend Helen suggested—no, she demanded that I go with her to a nearby city to visit her own optometrist. Dr. Stevens listened carefully to my narrative, performed the now despised "number" test, and then used what he called a "split-lens" instrument to view each eye.

He paused. He took a deep breath, exhaled, and in a most gentle manner, spoke. "I am so sorry to tell you this. But, I strongly believe you have corneal edema—a kind called Fuch's Dystrophy. It's an inherited condition that begins ever so slowly, then, progresses rapidly in its course. There is swelling of your corneas, and that swelling has been gradually destroying your vision. The corneal fluid cannot pass—be pumped—from one layer of cells to the next and back. I think... I think there's little time until you lose your vision completely. You need to see a cornea specialist as soon as possible. And, it so happens that a superb surgeon is down in Columbus. I know this sounds awfully rushed; but, will you allow me to call him right now?" It was my turn to pause. Then, I mutely assented to Dr. Stevens' request.

Two days later, Chuck, a department colleague, drove me to meet Dr. Johnson in Columbus, Ohio. Despite Chuck's attempts at humor, negativity, depression, and dejection dominated that three-hour trip. Those dark feelings changed, however, when I met the highly-regarded, highly-skilled ophthalmologist. During and following his examination of my eyes, he calmly assured me that I could, and should have hope about seeing clearly again. And, that hope centered on the successful surgery and healing of cornea transplants. The process for renewing my vision, however, would be physically long and emotionally trying many times.

"Waiting" is one word that provides a way to describe the years of "times." December 1993... waiting for cornea tissue to become available. January 1994... waiting for the transplant surgery to occur. February-March 1994... waiting for the transplant "to take"—to begin to heal. April 1994... waiting in fear when the first transplant in the right eye was rejected. May-June 1994... waiting for another cornea and for another major surgery on my 50th birthday on July 1st, 1994. Then… waiting as the transplant for the right eye healed and each of twenty-four stitches was removed during a lengthy ten-month period.

However, the waiting did not cease. The eye surgeon now focused his skills on the left eye. Thus, waiting for another cornea, for a third transplant surgery, for nine-ten months of healing, and the extensive period of time to remove each of the twenty-four stitches took place a second time. During all this waiting, I began to believe I could write, direct, and star in my own soap opera, "As the Eye Heals." Or, I thought I might create a dark movie, "The Good Eye, the Bad Eye, and the Ugly Eye."

"Thanks" is another word appropriate for those years. There never can be sufficient gratitude for each and every person, and cat, who gave of themselves so unselfishly to help me during those first years of losing and of slowly regaining my sight. Certain people deserve high praise for what they did. The Ohio Northern University Academic Vice-President, and the Communication Arts Department chairman quietly and effectively procured medical leaves- of-absence for me quarter after quarter. Dave and Jane Weimer, compassionate retirees from the Physics Department and from Heterick Memorial Library, insisted on driving me from Ada to Columbus for my surgeries and follow-up visits. I lost count of the trips, each punctuated with a restaurant stop for anxiety-reducing warm pecan rolls covered in fresh butter. I lost count, too, of the grocery shopping trips provided by Rodi Underwood, and our daily jaunts to Hardee's Restaurant for hot, steaming coffee and a huge biscuit with fresh butter. It seems that "fresh butter" figured importantly in so many assists.

The personal touch from staff members of the Bureau of Services for the Visually Impaired (BSVI) left me in awe of what could be done to help me in daily functioning. Their arrangement for Books-on-Tape through the Cleveland Public Library made many potentially empty hours actually exciting. An Optilec Reader provided a way to "see" enlarged letters and words via its enclosed television camera. A large, battery-powered magnifying lens with a built-in-light, special lined note-paper, and easy-to-handle pens and pencils gave me a needed sense of confidence for writing I absolutely had to do. Identification of the stove top and oven controls and the dial on the telephone, seemingly small gestures, also made adjustment to the loss of vision easier.

And, there was one special, pewter-gray, furry-feline who gave unconditional love and support during the days and months of recovery. Thomas P. Cat (P. stood for Puddy) rarely left my presence—my lap. Though eating was vital to him, he was incredibly patient as I tried to provide the Science Diet kibbles and fresh water, without spilling either all over him or the tile floor. At night, he slept at my feet as though guarding against further darkness. Thomas and so many beautiful friends were always there figuratively providing light for me.

Finally, the battle for sight during the 1990s was over. Oh, I had to wear glasses, but that seemed a minor inconvenience. They worked. Just days after I was outfitted with them, I was asked to speak at a Recognition Dinner for faculty and staff who had served ONU for twenty-years. I felt honored to give tribute to our department chair and never-failing supporter of me. The speech was both serious and humorous as I—and Ohio Northern University—noted the fine gentleman's myriad accomplishments. The laughter and the applause, at so many moments, were not only for him, but also for my own newly-sighted achievement.

The eye surgeon and his staff, my friends and acquaintances, one small cat, and I had won. I felt somewhat impervious to any more vision problems. I returned to the classroom to teach persuasion, communication theory, and to direct the public speaking program. Once again, I adapted various forms of literature for Readers Theatre productions. There were emotional issues that plagued me in the ensuing years; however, my vision remained, literally, strong and clear.

Time passed into the 21st century. In 2003, in May, I elected to leave my life of thirty-years as a professor at Ohio Northern University. I retired. During the summer months, I planned and plotted what I happily called "my retirement trip." On September 1st, 2003, my navy-blue Dodge Neon and I left Ada, Ohio, for what became an adventure across eight states.

That trip to visit old friends and colleagues had a life of its own. Literal fear was ever present as I and my shaky Neon encountered large cars, bigger SUVs, and huge 18-wheelers on the Interstates ripping up the road at 75-80 miles-per-hour. However, that gut-wrenching fear did diminish at each stop for warm, caring visits. I felt joy and peace in northern New Mexico within the Southwest-Native-American and Hispanic arts and culture. I knew excitement in exploring high mountain passes, and in viewing wondrous, stunning, gold fall foliage from the rear platform of the Durango-Silverton narrow-gauge train car. I smiled. I was happy. The inner-vision became calm and contented. The outer-vision shouted I could see everything in vivid high-definition colors.

Arrival in Denver, Colorado, on October 1st, signaled a trip half-over. The return trip to Ohio lay before me. However, the pleasant anticipated visit with Gary and Karen, younger brother and sister-in-law, took form in an unusual, dramatic way. Scene: Gasping for air. Rising Action: Trip to emergency room for countless tests. Climax: Diagnosis and Admission for pulmonary embolism. Final Scene: Days in a hospital bed watching heparin drip into a vein.

All of this fear-inducing activity brought on a new view of my life. I saw myself dying during my trip, inadvertently killing others on the road. Where was my life going? For October and November, Gary and Karen urged me to remain with them, not only to recover my health, but also to consider moving from Ohio, purchasing a home, and renewing my status as a Colorado native. Serious commitment ensued. A perfect condo piqued my interest—and pocket book. I had found my home.

By December, the Ohio life had ended. A few carefully chosen items were traversing the country in the care of United Van Lines. Good-byes were made, and on the wintery night of December 13th, 2003, my eight-year-old feline-friend, Pipkin, and I arrived at Denver International Airport, and shuttled our way to my Lakewood condo. I saw Gary waiting for us, saw and felt the beauty and warmth of pine logs burning in the fireplace, and saw a small evergreen tree cleverly decorated for the holidays... saw Pipkin and me finally at home. More than pleased, we—the kitty and I—examined all the accoutrements. New bed. New appliances. New furniture. New barrister bookcases in the loft. New... litterbox.

My vision knew no boundaries. The title of the song, "I Can See Clearly Now." became my mantra. The days, the years moved along swiftly and smoothly until... There's always an "until." I awoke to what was to be a bright, sunny morning on January 24th, 2004. Within minutes I phoned Gary. I needed help immediately. I had no sight in my right eye, and I feared that vision in the left eye might also become blurred. A quick visit to Gary's optometrist merited a referral and a rapid drive to Denver Eye Surgeons to meet Dr. Todd Maus.

Hyphemas. Blood clots in my right eye had caused blindness. I learned that the condition could occur suddenly and, then, disappear gradually over days—sometimes even hours. Fear revolving around vision issues crept into my thoughts and feelings once again. Although I could drive legally with sight in one eye, I did not know when hyphemas would appear in the right eye, or in the left. My uncertainty meant the need to obtain rides through services offered by the City of Lakewood, and the Senior Resource Center. Taxi service for trips beyond the range of the agencies was costly, but incredibly reliable. Rueben and Barbara, two Metro Taxi drivers, provided a personal service for me.

Months passed and the hyphema condition expanded into other vision difficulties. Surgeries for cataract removal and for lens exchange were performed. Accepting the problems was… Well, there was never acceptance as fear held its course. I desperately wanted to see, not vague features, but bold vivid ones. Those words were almost a litany in my mind of what I wanted from my eyes—from my vision.

As can happen with cornea transplants, mine "wore out." Too much trauma meant the corneas from the Ohio surgeries would need to be replaced. Dr. Rajiv Kumar, the cornea specialist at Denver Eye Surgeons, began the transplant process at 6:30 a.m., April 7th, 2008—fourteen years from the first transplant in Ohio. Techniques had advanced. Now there were only fifteen sutures. Now there was outpatient surgery. Yet, nine-to-ten months of healing still had to take place before glasses could be made to augment my vision. That time-frame repeated two more times.

A retinologist performed a vitrectomy to enter the eye to remove vitreous which had become like firm-to-solid Jell-

O. A gas, instilled to help the eye hold it shape, slowly dissipated as new vitreous fluid formed. Months went by slowly during which healing occurred. After that interval, I returned to Dr. Kumar's care for the last surgery—the cornea transplant for the left eye. Waiting, again, was the dominant word.

To obtain the Best Corrected Visual Acuity (BCVA), I was fitted with hybrid contact lenses with a hard center surrounded by a soft skirt. Otherwise, given the distance from the eye to the plane of any glasses, I fought blurriness, ghosting, and double vision. When Tom Willis, the Denver Eye Surgeons' contact lens specialist, first inserted the hybrid lens, I was astonished. It was difficult to accept what appeared in that moment. The eye chart was white, not light gray, and every letter and number had an intense black, sharp, knife-edge quality. I could, for the first time in more than two decades, actually see clearly.

And so, a professional and caring relationship with the eye surgeons and their skilled technical staff has continued. They are there when my fears reach forward and then recede as sea foam on a sandy beach.

⌒

Recounting times of seeing and times of not seeing has granted clarity in assessing my life. The fear—yes, let's call it fear—that has held sway far too often in the literal realm of vision has also marked many of my feelings, thoughts, and actions in figurative ways. With insight provided by the distance of years, I recall in the following pages events, places, and people. These are "glimpses" of and into my life. Perhaps reading about them may help clarify past, present, and future elements in your life.

Please, do remember that the glimpses are what happened, what was seen, what was felt, what was believed from my point-of-view—from my perspective. The glimpses are, above all, mine.

ON BEING
YOUNG

There is no doubt that every adoptive family has a unique story surrounding the addition of a child into its life. I always knew I was "adopted," and I proudly shared that "title" with anyone I met. What is written here is a glimpse of a story—of my mother Elaine and me. The events encompassing my adoption were shared with me by my father and especially by my "Aunt" Vera, as I grew to adulthood. Vera also gave me beautifully-scripted letters written by Elaine on ftne vellum. The letters told of my growing ability to walk, of my constantly scuffing my little shoes, of my rolling in the lush grass with "Queenie," the golden collie I had been given. Vera's own letters to me expressed time and time again the love Elaine held for me. However, on August 29, 1948, I—her four-year-old daughter — could utter only, "My mommy... where is my mommy?" That day, my mommy had suddenly, unexpectedly died. She and I knew each other but a short time. She had smiled and I had giggled.

Our Daughter Is Home

She waved to her husband from the window of the Denver and Rio Grande train as it slowly moved from the station platform in Monte Vista to begin its trek to Denver, Colorado. Her name was Elaine. His was Harold. When the couple learned that they could never give birth to children, Elaine and Harold first acquired a little boy, now a two- year-old toddler. Then, early in 1944, they began the process of seeking to adopt another child. This time it was to be a little girl. Months passed. It seemed there were endless forms to complete and papers to sign before an infant would be available. In early December of 1944, the call came. All was ready. They were to come to Denver immediately to get their newborn child. As the couple readied to leave, serious complications developed with some of the cattle on their ranch in the San Luis Valley in southern Colorado. Harold wanted to postpone the trip; but, Elaine insisted that she go ahead and take the train alone. So, on a wintery, snowy, December morning, she listened to the creaking and groaning of the two locomotives pulling the train in its difficult, steep, ascent over the 14,000- foot-high Sangre de Christo mountain range.

Elaine tried to occupy herself—reading baby magazines, knitting an infant cap, writing a letter—but it was all to no avail. She kept staring out the train car window, or rather her reflection in it. She saw events in her life. Her friends at J.C. Penny's had laughed and teased her endlessly, when she first saw Harold, and frankly stated, "I'm going to marry that man." She saw their ever more frequent meetings at church, at bridge parties, at picnics. They would often drive between stands of dark-green pine trees winding their way up a narrow dirt road with its sharp switchbacks and drop-offs to get to Metros Lake, quietly, almost secretly, nestled in the high San Juan mountains. She saw herself wearing the stylish slacks of the late 1930s, topped with a white, silk, notched-collar blouse. She saw them trying to fish from the old, wooden dock of the Eagle Cabin; but, what they caught were laughter and kisses. They were in love.

A jolt of the train brought Elaine back to the winter present. She stood to stretch, walked the length of the railcar, returned to her cushioned seat. Again her thoughts drifted to times past—to the marriage in the small, artist community of Taos, New Mexico, where she and Harold knelt on a brilliant blue, yellow, and white Navajo rug. They sealed their vows as they drank wine from a double-spouted, pottery wedding vase crafted in the San Ildefonso Pueblo. Old men and women smiled in happiness for them as the couple strolled with arms wrapped around one another through the intimate art galleries, and around the ancient Spanish plaza.

Scenes of the past flowed into the future—a future with her daughter-to-be growing from an infant in her yellow snuggle-sack into a toddler. She imagined blue and pink frilly dresses, little turned-down scalloped socks in white Mary Jane shoes, a perky straw hat complete with ribbons, and, of course, small white gloves. She was going to love that baby—her special little girl. Elaine knew she and Harold would now have another child to love, to care for, to watch grow.

The slowing entrance of the train into Denver caused reality to intrude on Elaine's imagining. When Union Station came into view, and the train whistled its arrival, Elaine could not hold back her excitement. Indeed, she almost flew into the arms of her dearest friend. Vera Griffin was waiting for her. "Vera... Vera! We have to go to the Home right now." The friendship forged over the years allowed Vera to gently calm Elaine and convince her to wait a bit, to rest, to eat, and to review the final papers for the adoption. Only when Vera promised to take her to the Home that afternoon, did Elaine relent.

The "Home" to which Elaine referred was an orphanage for the unwanted and abandoned. Of course, getting the boys and girls adopted was the primary goal of the institution. Unfortunately, there were never enough potential parents-to-be. Thus, some children spent their lives at the Home until they reached adulthood, could find jobs, and live on their own. This was the place where Elaine was to receive her newborn, infant daughter. That afternoon, as promised, Vera and Elaine arrived at the Home. When they climbed the broad steps and entered the tan brick building, Elaine almost could not contain herself. In fact, she was effusive when they entered the reception area.

"We're here.... I'm here to get my little daughter!" "And, just who might you be?" queried the receptionist. "I'm Elaine... Elaine Roberts...

from the San Luis Valley... from Monte Vista. Harold—my husband—and I are adopting a baby!" "Ah, yes... I see." The receptionist consulted her appointment book. "Please be seated. I will notify the matron. I'm sure she will be with you in a while.... And, you said your name was Roberts?" "Yes, yes, of course." Elaine eagerly responded. The receptionist disappeared behind large, tall, walnut, double-doors. To Elaine and to Vera, her absence seemed interminable. When she did return, she coldly stated, "You may come with me, now."

Elaine and Vera were ushered down a long hallway, and finally into a well-appointed office with an imposing mahogany desk with stacks of papers and files. Beside it stood the matron—tall, thin, stern and somewhat hawkish. She swiftly motioned to the stiff-back chairs in front of the desk. "Please be seated." Then, after checking a file on his desk, the Home administrator—a contrast to the matron with his portly physique and black-vested suit—looked up. "Mrs. Roberts?" "Yes, sir." He was a man for whom "sir" was most appropriate. "Yes, sir.... I'm Elaine Roberts. And, this is my friend Vera Griffin." The gentleman turned back to the file, skimmed it again, then, peered over his glasses. "Mrs. Roberts,... I'm afraid we have some unpleasant news.... It's about the adoption..." "But, sir," Elaine interrupted. "We have filled out the forms. All the papers are in order. Just tell me what I need to sign now!" "Please, Mrs. Roberts, please, just a moment. This issue is not about the paperwork." "What then?" Panic rose in Elaine's voice. "Mrs. Roberts, the infant you were to adopt, to take with you today, is ill—gravely ill. During the infant's last examination, our physician determined her severe jaundiced condition is chronic. She is too ill to leave this Home. We simply cannot release the child for adoption." "But, why didn't you..." "I'm sorry, Mrs. Roberts, but we could not reach you or your husband to tell you not to come." "But I'm here. I am here, now!" Elaine was becoming more and more agitated. Vera put her arm around her. "Elaine, honey, it'll be OK." "No, Vera, it's not OK. I came here for my daughter. I won't leave without her!"

"Mrs. Roberts!" the matron spoke sharply. "It's just not possible. You're going to have to accept it. There is no newborn for you to adopt." Frantically speaking through a rush of tears, Elaine begged, "Isn't there something you can do? Isn't there a new baby?" Again the matron began, "Mrs. Roberts... please!" The administrator rose, and gently spoke, "I know you're upset, and I certainly can understand why. This is most difficult for you. But, right now, before you leave, would you like just to see and say hello to some of our children?" It was an obvious attempt to assuage Elaine's dismayed feelings which were hurting like an open wound. "No... I'd rather not." "Oh, why not, dear?" Vera quickly asked. "It would be a nice thing to do."

The administrator nodded to the matron. Both escorted Elaine and Vera to a large room, a nursery filled with several rows of cribs. Some children were whimpering, some crying, as two attendants circulated among these older infants. Fighting back more tears, Elaine began to walk slowly among the cribs. She tried to smile at the children, but her despair wouldn't leave, until... until she came to a crib with a little girl who hesitantly turned her head to look at this person. Elaine stopped, smiled warmly, and winked at the little one. The child looked at her and giggled. In a special, a magic sort of moment, the two of them locked eyes. They grinned at one another. And, the child reached out to Elaine with her small, grasping hands. Without a second thought, Elaine bent down, embraced the child, and turned to Vera, to the matron, and to the administrator. "This child, this little girl... I want her to be my daughter."

"But, Mrs. Roberts," interjected the matron, "she's six-months-old. She acknowledges no one. Since she was born, she has never cried, never laughed, nor made any sound until this moment. She cannot be adopted. She is what we call an unadoptable." She wanted to continue; but, the administrator firmly hushed the matron. There was a studied silence. Then, he smiled and spoke gently. "I think we can arrange for this child to become your daughter, if you wish." "Oh, I do, I do! Just look at her. See, Vera, see her hazel eyes, her red hair. Oh, the way she looks at me, it's…" She had no more words.

Elaine would not let go of the child. She held her close as they made their way back to the administrator's office. "All we have to do is change a few items on all the forms, and have you sign them. If we are in agreement with all the requirements again, you may be able to take the little one with you today." The matron huffed off to gather what few items had been used for the child. Noting this, Elaine reminded Vera, "Oh, I have blankets and everything she'll need for the trip home." She reluctantly allowed Vera to hold the now napping child as she turned to complete the paperwork. "Sir… may I ask, what was her birth-mother like?" "Mrs. Roberts, you know that information is sealed forever.…. You are now her mother—her only mother." Elaine paused. Then, "Thank you, oh thank you for those words.…. Thank you with all my heart for permitting me to meet—to find—our new child. May I… may I phone my husband? Harold should know right away." She called and reached him quickly. "Yes, dear, I know you've been waiting to hear.…. Sh-sh, now. I'll explain later. Just know that I am holding our little, six-month-old, curly-red- haired, daughter. I know she's anxious to meet you.…. Yes, I'm with Vera now, but I'll be on the next train. See you soon, my dear… And, we both love you!"

Elaine and the child spent the night hours in each other's arms. With loving farewells made to Vera, who had suddenly become "Aunt" Vera, Elaine and the little girl departed Union Station in early morning snow flurries. In the warmth of the compartment, her new daughter immediately fell asleep with the rocking of the train car. Elaine sighed, feeling her own exhaustion and anxiety slip away. She gently whispered, "You will be named after your daddy's wonderful mother, and after my wonderful mother, darling little one."

The creaking of the train cars, the piercing sound of an engine's whistle, disturbed neither Elaine nor the child. The slow journey up the mountains was just that—slow. It seemed that the laboring locomotives would never get them to Monte Vista. After long, long hours, the train finally reached its destination—and the destination for Elaine and the child. Snuggly holding the little one, Elaine made her way to the passenger car door, and ever so carefully stepped down to meet her husband—the new father of the child. Their little daughter, now wide awake, smiled brightly, and grinned at him. What followed were tears and hugs... and love.... Elizabeth Ann was home.

Sense of confusion—a questioning. Sense of need—a hungering.
Sense of aloneness—an aching.
Sense of love—only momentary. Sense of loss—loving gone.
Sense of emptiness—forever.

Abandoned

She knows a special world. She knows thoughts. She knows motion. She feels warmth. She senses time. She hears sounds which become intense noise. This causes distress in her. Once gentle movements become uncomfortable jerks. Then suddenly, too suddenly, she feels sharp pain. She gasps and inhales shocking, cold air. She sees extreme light. Her eyes express surprise with salty, bitter tears. Then, something tight encompasses her in this alien place. Something takes her from the brightness. There is no sound from the something, no sound from her. She feels abruptly placed in a small, tight, confined space. The something moves away. She becomes aware of different, louder sounds from somewhere nearby. She, however, utters no sound. She seeks refuge from all sensations around her. She closes her eyes, dreams of floating warmth.

Harsh squalling awakens her, jolts her from her shadow world. She becomes aware of large forms somewhere nearby. The figures make soft shushing sounds. But, not one figure comes to her. She lies motionless until a figure gives her a warm liquid which she suckles from some pliable thing. It and the liquid provide peace as she watches. She is moved only to take away her wetness, then returned to her restricting place. Afterward, there is nothing, no forms, no one. She sleeps to wake alone. Inside, deep inside, she experiences loss. She has been taken from what was a comforting somewhere to what is nowhere. At that point, her fragile being senses she is terribly alone.

Time, as she grasps it, passes from light to dark, from dark to light. Only one or two forms come to her in the light periods. She hears a sound, "milk," which she begins to identify with the soothing liquid brought to her. But, the long absence of forms makes her feel an interminable aching. Though fragile, she grows. She now equates the sound, "people," with those forms she sees for only brief moments. "Food" also enters her knowledge of the sphere around her. Her small self now wears white cotton shirts and white cotton diapers. She is quiet and almost motionless except when the emptiness surrounding her brings moist eyes and an inner silent whimpering as sleep overcomes dark fears.

The child, who entered the world on Independence Day, has no freedom, however, from the daily, dull, mundane existence, now in a larger place. Here there is a "crib." She learns that word when those she no longer senses as unidentifiable forms place her in it. Days, weeks, and months pass by as she looks around the room in mute attendance. She has now been in this world for six long months.

One day, when the sense of loss hurts so deep inside, something different happens. A new person, a lady, she thinks, with tears in her own eyes, stands beside her crib. The child turns to her and their sadness joins. In one captivating, extraordinary moment, smiles come. The child's hazel-colored eyes brighten, mimicking the radiant eyes of the lady. The little one utters a sound—a giggle—the first sound she has ever made. The lady gives a small cry, carefully picks up the child, draws her close, and hugs her ever so gently. Words are whispered to the child, "I will be your Mommy, now. You are my little red-haired, curly-headed girl. Oh, please know, please understand, I will love you forever."

And... she does love the child. And... the little one does love her mommy. Days and months pass again. However, this is time filled with warmth, caring, chats, hugs, kisses, rides, walks, and most of all love. It is time filled with yellow, with pink, with white. Frilly dresses, soft fuzzy coats, shiny Mary Jane shoes clothe the child. And, a wet-nosed golden collie nudges her to play. All this surrounds her until one day.....

"Mommy? Where's my mommy?... I want my mommy." The plaintive words are barely audible as the little girl slowly, step by step, climbs down the stairs. Her fingers lightly grasp the smooth, burnished, walnut bannister. The four-year-old child slowly enters the living-room of the place she knows as home. She has been searching and searching the second floor rooms. The small one has walls of brightly-printed yellow daisies. The bed, dresser, and shelves are special, just her size. The large one with its bed, so tall, covered with a soft, deep-red, comforter and pillows is mommy's room. The little girl has not found what she has been looking for. Not in the hallways. Not in the rooms. Not in the dark closets.

At the bottom of the stairs, she asks again, "Mommy? Where is my mommy?" Her quiet, wondering, little voice is lost among the murmuring sounds of other voices. There is a subdued atmosphere as she finds her way from living room to dining room. Once again, she utters, "Where is my mommy?" There is no answer to her query from the tall people all dressed in black. She weaves through them, and receives an occasional pat on her curly hair, but no response to her questions.

The small one wanders slowly among the black forest of legs. Under her breath, she continues her question, "Mommy… Where is my mommy?" An idea comes to her. Perhaps Mommy is not in the house. She walks with a renewed sense of purpose to the glassed-in white porch. No tall people are here, so she slowly reaches for the door knob, turns it, opens the door, and slips out onto the stone walk. The sun shines brightly in contrast to the shadowy gray inside the house. With hope, she moves across the lawn toward the entrance and the high fence. Taught early not to go beyond the wrought-iron gate, the little girl pauses, and calls, "Mommy." No answer. She wants to cry, but no tears come.

Turning away from the imposing gate, the little girl runs toward the old orchard with its craggy, apple tree branches. There in the tall, waving, emerald-green grasses she searches and searches. "Where are you, Mommy? Come push me high!" She climbs onto the smooth, wooden seat of the thick rope swing. "Push me higher and higher, Mommy!" No response. The disconsolate child sits rocking back and forth in silence. The grasses sway, as if in accompaniment. Then, she slips off the swing to hug her big, gold and white collie. The dog has come to her to assuage the child's sadness. As she tightly grasps the long, silky fur, she asks, "Where is my mommy?" The collie gives only gentle nuzzles and licks on her cheeks. She leans on the collie's shoulder and slowly walks back toward the gloom inside the house where she has known only unconditional love.

From the sunny porch to the darkened living room, she wanders again, still seeking "Mommy." Dejected and alone, she finally sits on the soft, cushioned sofa. Someone beside the little girl touches a lace-edged handkerchief to damp eyes. Sensing a palpable sorrow surrounding this older woman, the child hesitantly moves to her to ask, "Where is my mommy?" The woman places an arm around her and draws her close to her bosom. She quietly tells the child that her mommy is no more. The little one whispers only, "Mommy? Where is my Mommy? I want my Mommy."

Sometimes when we return to thoughts of the past, we may recall,
with deep pain, events which hurt today as much as yesterday.

She Has Done It Again

She has done it again.

The words beat and repeat like a vicious, haunting echo.

She—There were the myriad natures in her disposition.

I lost count long ago.

It—There were the two-letter, grain-of-a-pronoun, occasions almost insignificant, but not.

I lost count long ago.

Again—There were the always recurring times of love, hate, non-acknowledgment.

I lost count long ago.

A beginning. Almost six. She entered my life.

A life, a war-torn world.

Loss of birth mother. Loss of adopted love. Loss of tender innocence.

Now, a hope of happiness when She was to wed Daddy.

But: "You sit. You stay there. You be quiet. You don't wrinkle that dress." Preceded ceremony.

In her home was the joining, Rowing with white.

White ribbons. White candles. White-upon-white Rowers.

Tears came. Memory came. White array of white when "Mommy-Elaine" died.

I do not like white.

Crept from stiff bench. Hid behind Grandfather's soft-cushioned chair.

Then, reluctant, went for picture-taking with brother, daddy, Her.

"You crumpled your dress." Said firmly.

"Smile, now, honey." Said sweetly.

"Smile, or else." Said.

Late night. Dark. Arrived at our ranch home.

Taken. Half-marched to my upstairs' room.

"Get out of that dress. Icing from my cake is on it. You won't ever wear it again."

She turned to leave. Stopped abruptly.

"You know I love you, sweetheart. Happy dreams."

I said nothing.

＿＿＿

Next morning call. "Hurry up! Get down here and eat."

Corn Rakes. Cold milk. Left for me.

Daddy and brother gone for outside chores.

Awkward silence.

"You must call me 'Mommy' from now on."

Jolt. Confusion. My "Mommy" was still Mommy-Elaine.

Deep sadness. Memory of terrible loss, too close in time.

She intruded into my life.

I said nothing.

New directive. "Help me get rid of this stuff!"

Hour after hour. Room after room. Attacked for china, doilies, towels. And, framed pictures.

All boxed for storage. Somewhere.

Dinner prepared. Felt queasy during meal. Could not eat.

"Go to your room. No playing. Just sit."

Then: Heard them. Tempers Rared. Voices argued.

"I want them to remember her." Pleading.

"Sure, put her picture out. Put it on the piano. But... if you do, I will leave.

You can be alone—with your picture and two kids!"

Choice made. Morning came. "Mommy-Elaine" was gone.

July 1. Sixth birthday. New-Mommy made beautiful cake.

Angel food. White icing. Green leaves. Red roses. Pink candles.

"Happy Birthday" song. Clapping. Cheering.

Presents: -Bright red lunch pail for fall school

-Big boy doll in yellow knit clothes

-Pretty pictures in fairy-tale book

-Little green John Deere toy tractor

-Roy Rogers cap-pistol and holster

Thank you and hugs. All happy ranch girls needed a six-shooter.

New-Mommy disapproved of tom-boy toy.

I said nothing.

⌐◦

July 2. Strapped on "Roy Rogers." Went to show new gun to foreman's twins.

I did not hear her follow. Grabbed arm. Half-dragged into house.

"What do you think you're doing? Give me that gun. You'll never see it again!

You should play with your doll from your Grammy."

In my room. Looked at doll. Remembered "Roy Rogers."

⌐◦

August time. Warm, loving, day with Grandmother R. Took boy doll with yellow outfit. We played.

Surprise for me. Grandmother made clothes for doll.

Bright blue shirt. Red corduroy overalls. So nice. So fun.

Then: Drove home with New-Mommy. Showed her doll with new clothes.

"Wasn't the outfit Grammy gave you good enough? You'll never play with that doll again!"

I said nothing.

⌐◦

School Day 1. Lunch box prepared. Surprise chocolate-chip cookies. Walked to bus. Hugs and kisses.

Excited. Happy. Good day. End of special day came. Ran from bus to share experiences.

Added numbers. Read "Dick and Jane." Played with new friends.

Then: "I know where you were. You scuffed your shoes. Do you hear me? Don't do it again!"

But, shoes did get scuffed. On dirt playground. On slides. On swings.
On monkey-bars.

Heard anger. About it.

I said nothing.

—

Second Grade Class. Little red measles spots.

Missed teacher. Missed friends. Even missed Palmer Penmanship.

Warmly-wrapped in blankets. On living-room sofa.

She read comics from Denver Post.

She designed, cut, beveled leather to make billfold for me.

She put lucky-penny in coin pocket.

She smiled.

Then: "Don't you ever lose it!" I did not.

—

Third Grade Class. Mumps to each kid.

Confusing stay at home. In bed. Drawn curtains.

"You just lie there. Don't you even listen to the radio!"

Questions to self: Had I done a terrible wrong? Was I punished for
"it"—again?

Back to class: Made "A-s" in all subjects. "D" in deportment.

Saw her Anger. Fury. Shame. Accused of "not paying attention."

I had quietly talked to friend—imaginary.

Friend and I introduced to Her razor-strap. Asked what it was for.

I learned. Whipped only by her. No one knew.

"You'd better get used to this if you keep being bad."

Didn't know exactly what this "bad" meant.

I tried not to be that.

⌒͎

Then: Talked to Friend only as sleep came. I dreamed of "wild, black horse"

in corral.

People-She warned me to keep away.

But, thought… I will show love to the horse. The horse will love me.

No. Not in this dream.

Was stomped into dirt. Lifeless. Dead.

People-She showed Caring. Remorse. Sadness.

Fantasy repeated each night… every night.

Then: Darkness…. And thought….

Death brought love.

Much to consider. Again and Again and Again.

*There are moments of sheer, downright fun we experience as children. Later
in our lives, we may recall and see such moments with unadulterated joy. We
may also remember and see such moments with an aching sadness and sorrow.*

New Mown Hay

I used to love new mown hay. I was a child then.

Hay was to smell, to feel, to dive into.

Tall, rectangular, pale-green haystacks dotted the landscape in the summer.

In the meadows, near the corrals, beside the barn.

Double-dares with brother to jump into the haystack.

Forty-feet from the second-story door of the barn.

No fear of high places.

Belly-flop dives into the fresh hay, screaming with freedom.

Using hands, arms, legs, feet to swim to the edge.

Slide down off the hay fast and faster.

So proud, repeat and repeat the dive-swim-slide routine.

Until—sudden stop.

Father watching our play, seeing haystack slump.

Flash of anger in his eyes, in his voice.

Standing stock-still, then removing leather belt with metal buckle and tip.

Slapping thigh, determined to punish.

We want to run for pitchforks.

We want to fix the haystack.

We want to be good.

Not to be.

Must bare bottoms, must feel pain of leather and metal.

Must watch him walking away, hear him cursing away.

Fond thoughts are there no more.

I used to love new mown hay.

Equus caballus, i.e., Horse: A large solid-hoofed
herbivorous mammal, used… for riding.

Equestrian Days

I don't remember when my affection for horses began. I always cherished the idea of being an equestrian; although, at age five, I may have had only a vague grasp of the word. For me, loving horses was easy. They were right there on our ranch in southern Colorado. Even though I knew about horses from nose to withers, flank to tail, certain elements of my riding career were less than successful.

I admit my childhood brought limitations. I needed a step-stool to reach the backs of the horses for brushing and combing. For that task, I was judged as tall enough. Yet, for slipping on a bridle, and putting on a saddle, I was judged as not tall enough. I disliked the latter judgment which implied I couldn't have my own horse. I needed a horse—be it black, brown, sorrel, buckskin, or pinto—in order to be a real "horseperson." But, my parents simply stated, "You're not good enough to have a horse of your own." Such judgment regarding my competency applied to myriad other tasks and events throughout my life. However, as far as my equestrian days are concerned, I now observe a notable few with bittersweet clarity.

"Smokey and the Cows"

One of my early riding adventures as a somewhat immature five-and-a-half-year-old involved a broad-backed, slow- moving, large gray horse. Being a skilled (at least I thought I might be) rider of horses, I slipped onto Smokey's bare back as he stood next to a corral fence and dozed in peaceful reverie in the mid-afternoon sun. My sneaky movement startled him, and he began a jerky jaunt from the corral to the pasture. At that moment in my journey, I still thought myself quite adept with this horse, even though I was sitting on his back without benefit of saddle-horn, let alone a saddle, and without benefit of the reins of a bridle. The wobbly walk (I was the wobbly one.) through the open corral gate gave me a bit of concern. I was a short kid, thus, I had short legs. Because Smokey's back was so wide, my legs didn't fit down around his shoulders. So, there was no way to grasp, or to hang onto him with my knees. My legs and feet stuck out from Smokey's back like little wings.

Usually the big old gray horse plodded his way through life. That afternoon, he broke into a semi-trot, and headed across the pasture to where our Jersey and Guernsey milk-cows grazed on the rich, green grass. I now became the bouncing one, and grabbed a shank of Smokey's dark-gray mane in an effort to stabilize my small frame. A vision of falling off spun in my mind. I shouted "Whoa, Smokey!" Nothing. I yelled "Whoa!" four, five, six more times. Smokey ignored me, and with his odd gait made it to the corner of the pasture. By this time, I was flat on his back, face-in-mane, knowing I was going to slide from Smokey's back into slushy, muddy, grassy, water, and be chased by four angry cows. I was short, and they were at least fifteen-feet-tall—to me. One swishy swipe of a tail, and I'd be a goner. After all, I'd seen those wild-eyed, bucking bulls at a rodeo.

Smokey finally halted, too far from a fence for me to extricate myself from my dilemma. The complacent cows ignored me, as they contentedly chewed their cud. Smokey tossed his head and neck down to grab sprigs of grass, and chew at them. I no longer held onto his mane. I just sat on his back and sniffied at my dire straits. Then, as embarrassed as I was, I began to call for help, in a weak feeble way. No one responded. I shouted. I screamed. No one responded. "Daddy... Daddy! Help me." I sobbed. From where I sat on old Smokey, the barn and corrals were far more than a half-mile away. So, I sat. I cried. I hollered. The sequence was repeated over and over as the minutes passed into hours.

My hope that Daddy, or someone, anyone, would help me was turning to despair. Then in the distance, I saw a figure, carrying a large bucket. The figure kept approaching and banging on the bucket. I heard words that sounded like "C'mon cows—milkin' time! C'mon, c'mon. Come get your oats!" The figure strolled ever closer. Relief. It was my daddy. Almost voiceless now, I tried to yell, "Daddy, I'm here. Come get me!"

I tried to urge Smokey toward him; but, Smokey only ambled closer to mix with those darn milk-cows. And, then, the figure stopped. I could see his face at this point. He grinned, and started to chuckle. That grew into full-blown amusement. I was shocked. I was crushed. I had been stuck on this stubborn beast for over two hours, and this man, my father, who was supposed to care for me, was bent over convulsed in thigh-slapping laughter. "Daddy, help me." I weakly called. I still held a smidgeon of hope for my rescue.

Instead, my father banged on the bucket again. The cows looked up from their grassy delicacies, and began to go toward him, to follow him across the pasture. It was milking time. Daddy was leaving. The only person to help me made no attempt to retrieve the horse or me. I was still alone on that dumb old horse which, like the cows, smelled the rolled-oats, shook his head, and followed them to the corral. Again, I had to hang on desperately. Near the barn, Smokey finally came close to a wood fence pole. I quickly grabbed it, and slid sideways off his huge, broad back.

Daddy took the cows on into the barn to their stalls, fed them some of the rolled-oats, sat down on the three- legged stool, and began the milking process. He never said a word. He just looked at me, and shook his head in a dismayed, discouraged, and displeased way. I slowly walked away in silence.

I did not go near that horse or those cud-chewing cows for a long, long time. I had been a really scared kid. Lack of concern and non-support that day hurt deeply. But when the humiliating pain eased, I still dreamed of being a superbly-skilled rider.

"Choices Do Count"

When I reached the age of eleven, I held to my desire to be exceptional at riding. I loved the horseback trips each summer to seek Native Brook Trout in the headwaters of a small stream nestled in the nearby San Juan Mountains. I loved simply brushing and combing the horses. I loved cleaning and polishing the saddles and bridles. I did not love sitting in the house learning to hand-stitch the hem of a dress for a 4-H sewing club. There I had to act like a young lady, and young ladies needed to be able to sew. Because I abandoned cooking club endeavors two years before, and joined a livestock club, making a dress was now chosen as a goal I had to achieve. The goal was not mine, however. My step-mother took ownership of that.

With all that in mind, I pictured "Choice # 1"—an August day, a cool breeze, the sound of a horse neighing, and the opportunity to ride the horse. I pictured "Choice # 2"—an August day, no breeze, a partially constructed, ugly, brown and rose patterned dress, and the chance to sew the hem of said dress. After much difficult comparison (about as long as it took the mother-figure to head our car toward town), I made "Choice # 1."

I dumped aside the offensive dress, and ran to the barn, grabbed a blanket, grabbed a saddle, grabbed a bridle, and coaxed "Dynamite" into letting me put all the gear on him. This black-and-white pinto displayed some side- stepping, antsy, behavior as I swung up onto the saddle. But, he did allow me to ride him to the dirt lane which led to the foreman's house. Dynamite set a good pace as he trotted up the lane. All was OK until Lucy and Laurie, the foreman's twins, began to run toward Dynamite, with me on board. Seeing the excited girls, jumping and waving, made Dynamite stop, lurch, whirl around—and buck. I tried to hang on. But, I bounced up high, flipped sideways, caught my foot in the right stirrup, and fell toward the ground. The thoroughly spooked Dynamite headed for the barn, bucking and kicking all the way. I was afraid he would kick my head, as my back and shoulders hit and dragged on the dirt. After what seemed an eternity, I finally twisted my foot out of the stirrup, and dropped to the ground.

The twins ran to get their father, as I crawled off the road into a muddy alfalfa field. When he came, he picked me up, and placed me rather ungraciously on the back bed of his truck. Not inside. Outside. He wanted no mud, or maybe no blood, in the cab. His concern "underwhelmed" me. Once unloaded at home, I tried to clean off the dirt to check the extent of my injuries.

Then, she—the sewing mom—arrived, and assessed the situation with a snarl. "What did you think you were doing? You're OK. Just clean up and get back to work on that dress! No excuses. No whining. You know what to do!" I kept my bruises and pain hidden. I set aside, almost buried, any hope to be a brilliant rider. Given similar circumstances, though, I hoped that I'd make the same choice again—without the kids, and the kicking.

Within a few days, I did complete the repulsive dress. It won First Place at the county fair. It won a Blue Ribbon as the state fair. I never wore the dress.

"Tootie and the Pie"

"Joyce Anne......" Her registered name went on at length—most impressive. Our family chose to call the addition to our collection of horses, "Tootie." This young horse had a beautiful, rich, sorrel color, with a striking, small, white blaze on her forehead. And, she was intelligent, eager to work, and incredibly sharp in her movements. Tootie was a quarter-horse that had the innate skill of her breed to cut out a cow or steer from the herd, almost by herself. She knew instinctively which way the animal would run to return to the herd, and she would pivot on her back legs and hooves in order to keep the animal on track. Her skill was an amazing sight to see. It was an art.

I almost drooled with desire to be on her back. My step-mother, who claimed Tootie as her own, offered a stern "No," again and again whenever I asked to ride the stunning horse. One afternoon, however, the "No"-person was away at a Rock Creek Social Club gathering. My father called to me while I was doing some lawn work, actually digging up dandelions. "Get over here to the barn. We've got to get moving to bring in a cow that has woody- tongue. She's over in the east pasture. And, the vet is on his way."

When I got to the barn, Dad was saddling his horse, "Spotty," a big, hulking, brown-and-white pinto, ridden only by him. He had already saddled Tootie. That could mean only one thing—I would be riding her! I grabbed the reins, and the saddle horn, and swung up gracefully onto the back of that wonderful horse. Within a few minutes, we had galloped to the pasture, and begun to slowly ride among the cattle to search for the sick cow. We were worried about her. A bit of fox-tail grass had lodged in the cow's mouth, causing huge swelling of her tongue, making it unable for her to eat or drink.

Tootie zeroed in on the cow immediately. And, without any effort on my part, she began to circle around the cow and nudge her toward the pasture gate. The sick cow complied. The return trip to the corral was so smooth that I slipped my boots from the stirrups, and clung to the saddle and horse with only my knees. Dad and Spotty, Tootie and I had moved the cow some distance when suddenly the cow broke away to run back to the herd.

In a fraction of a second, Tootie, with no guidance whirled to turn the cow back toward the open gate, where Dad and Spotty were now headed. The cow turned left to run. Tootie swerved left. The cow paused a second, then turned right. Tootie pivoted to the right, stopping the cow in its tracks. The lively moves were like an orchestrated dance, except that I—Miss Smart Ass Teenager—couldn't hang on with just my knees. Thus, when Tootie spun to the right, I flew to the left in a slow arc. I hit the grass with my back and butt, caught my breath, sat up and looked for Tootie beside me. In movie westerns, the hero's horse always came to aid the injured character. But, Tootie was gone. She had stayed with the sick cow, and already had herded her through the gate.

I called to my father. "Help me get Tootie! Get me back to the barn." He just sat there laughing. "What?" I yelled. He sneered, "I'm not coming near you." He pointed at me, and at the ground on which I still sat. "Oh, thanks, Dad. You're really great!" Then, the smell hit me. I had not only flown off Tootie and landed on the ground, but I had also landed in a brown, squishy, fresh, cow-pie. To add further insult to injury, Tootie had gone on and herded the cow to the barn—by herself. Dad and Spotty left me and trotted on to catch up to her. I had to walk back to the barn alone. At that point, I felt abandoned. I could only think that family support and kindness, and the hope to ride that horse ever again were long gone.

"Dream of a Better Time"

I believe my most accomplished riding skills took place, not in a grassy pasture, or in a rodeo arena, but in my dreams. Every night when I went to bed and snuggled under the warm covers, I closed my eyes and began one of my horse stories in my mind. In that world I created, and in which I held imagined conversations, I succeeded in all my endeavors.

The initial darkness in my mind's vision held voices that told me I hadn't been good enough, wasn't good enough, and would never be good enough to ride. I turned my face into the soft pillow where I sought refuge from the words that encompassed more than my ability to ride. I fought back tears. In my mind's scenario, I planned to fight negative laughter, sneers, disgust, and worst of all, non-acknowledgement that I existed.

There was an element of "I'll show you!" in my dream. Those who hurt me were wrong. I would squash their cynicism. The personal doubt I carried with me would also disappear. At the beginning of the scene, I would be in the middle of a corral surrounded by a high pole fence. Seated on the top rails were those who lacked confidence in me, who hesitated to stand with me, who sought to discredit me. The jeers from them made me ache. They stung like an open, festering wound. But, I turned around slowly and smiled warmly at each one. I felt vulnerable, but knew my smile was a way of disarming their attitudes.

The action began in my mind-thoughts. Someone called out, "Hey, stupid! Here's a challenge for you." With that dare, he threw open a gate, slapped a horse on the rump, and yelled, "Go stomp her to death!" I choked, fear knotted in my gut, and I almost slumped to the ground. The horse that charged into the ring was not a run-of-the- mill, gentle riding horse. This one towered far above me. The muscles of the stallion rippled with strength. His sharp hooves struck the ground like thunder. His whinny was an ear-splitting angry scream. The red eyes shone with rage. And, he was black, pitch-black, coal-black, raven-black. He was a devil horse.

In my imagined world, silence overcame my tormenting observers who gripped the top rail of the fence when the beast charged around the corral. I remained in the center of that space. Strength came. I stretched up all of my five- foot height, and carefully watched the horse's behavior. I saw the look of alarm on the faces of the fence-sitters as the black beast stomped and reared in front of them.

The scene continued. I began to feel that I knew that horse. The anger he outwardly displayed mirrored my inner turmoil which lay buried in fear of reprisals. The stallion slowed his dramatic circles around the corral, and turned to face me. I looked at his red eyes, not in fear, but in empathy. His look met mine. He reared, screamed, and charged at me. I did not move or hesitate to look at him. His hooves sliced the air and ground, as he came to a halt three feet from me. Our eyes were still locked. I spoke to him silently. I told him that I shared his pain. I understood the abuse he had endured, the abuse which drove the anger deep inside him.

In my mind-story, the magnificent creature relaxed, and literally dropped his neck and head, as he step-by-slow- step came to me. I held up my open hand which he nuzzled with his velvet-soft nose. With my other hand, I reached to stroke the glistening hair of his neck and mane. In my mind, the abusers on the corral fence sat numbly in silence.

This so-called devil horse was there as my guardian spirit. My horse paladin and protector knelt on his front legs. I knew what I was to do, and did not falter. I crossed to his side and slid onto his back. He lifted me up and stood to his full stature. Our heads turned to scan the abusers, then, turned away. I seemed as one with him and had no need to even grip his sides or mane. In one flowing, smooth motion, he began to gallop toward the stupefied ones—fast, faster, straight at them. Then, he leaped and hurled over them, our obstacles. He and I never touched ground again. As we rose, we left pain behind. We found our freedom, as we died to them.

I awoke from my mind-story. Tears, and with them a deep sadness, meant reality had once again broken into my dream.

There is an old tune, often sung at religious revivals, known as "Washed in the Blood of the Lamb." Now, should I have ever attended such an event, the behavior of my brother and me might have provoked another vocal entry for seeking repentance. We would have, indeed, been marked, castigated, and, thus, directed to see the light.

Marked by the Sin

The year was 1954. I was ten-years-old, a fifth-grader in Mrs. Harris's class at the elementary school in our hometown in Colorado. My brother Jim was eleven-years-old, a sixth-grader in Mrs. Meeker's class at the school noted above. Jim was seen as the not-so-quiet one, the less-than-innocent child. I was seen as the quiet one, the epitome-of-innocence child. Both of us were young and, innocent or not, saw humor where humor was seldom allowed. This information aids in examining two sacrilegious individuals, two who committed sin. The sin was seen. The sin was perpetrated in a church. The sin left them marked. All eyes of the congregation saw the marks. Punishment was the only means of exonerating their behavior. Disciplinary action would, according to custom, be meted out by the abashed parents.

Jim and I, the committers of the sin, were part of a family group— Father, Mother, little two-year-old Gary, Jim, and me. We five went to the local Methodist Church every Sunday. Such regularity of attendance was not due, perhaps, to strong belief in the tenets of John Wesley. It was due, most likely, to the fact that Father sang in the choir, and that he graced the congregation with solos in his remarkable tenor voice. Thus, our church-going was definitely an obligatory family affair.

Gary was always taken to the "Children's Room" in the basement of the church. During the service upstairs, he and others of his age played and slept. At ages eight and nine, Jim and I had served time in the "Room." As I recall, I think we were read questionably appropriate stories of Biblical material. The beheading of John the Baptist was a sensational, bloodcurdling, attention-getter story. David wholloping Goliath between the eyes also made for fascinating, gory study. These, and other stories, provided more violence than many television programs at that time.

However, at ages ten and eleven, Jim and I had matured enough to be allowed to sit through the "upstairs" church service. We had become "little adults," who had to sit on the hard, wooden pews with our respective parents, grandparents, and other assorted relatives. The Roberts had always sat together. The Roberts had always sat in the same pew. The pew was the second to the last row on the left-side of the center aisle. There was no bronze plaque that noted it was the Roberts' pew. It just was. Sitting on the left side of the large church congregation did not indicate my grandparents' nor my parents' political proclivities. No, they definitely thought they were correct in their right-leaning, conservative persuasion.

And so, attired in our Sunday-finery, Jim and I learned to sit through the church services. We heard our father's songs. We sang Charles Wesley's hymns. The latter allowed Jim and me the chance to stand, to become less twitchy. Then, we had to sit again. To survive, I focused on the organist who dozed off during the sermons. I focused on the difference between the American flag and the Christian flag. I focused on the letters carved into the front of the altar. I never knew what *In Hoc Signum* meant until eighth-grade Latin class. Methodists weren't too Latin- oriented in their teachings. However, the most interesting focal feature for me was the Communion rail and the little holes in it.

Communion, itself, was most intriguing. As little adults, Jim and I were allowed to partake in this monthly ritual in the church service. Select women from the "Ladies' Ruth Society" prepared everything for Communion. They snapped the white linen cloth into a triangle and placed it over the altar. They carefully draped the long, white linen cloth over the front of the altar-rail to which each member of the congregation would come, first-pew-first, to kneel to receive, in remembrance, the "Bread of Life" and the "Blood of Christ." The "bread" consisted of unleavened bits from some out-of-town bakery. The "blood" was Welch's grape juice which was served in tiny, extremely tiny shot- like glasses. There was never a sniff of wine in the teetotalling Methodist Church. Wine, the drink of the devil, was used by those Catholics across town.

Father would take early Communion with the choir. Our trio of Mother, Jim, and me were among the last in the congregation to proceed to the altar-rail for Communion. On that Sunday, as we knelt, the "Ladies" placed new Welch's grape juice glasses in the holes, and gave the minister a new plate of bread bits. Since I was at the beginning of the altar-rail, the minister came to me first. I took a minute square piece of the unleavened bread and put it in my mouth to chew during the appropriate words read by the minister, and during the tune of "Nearer My God to Thee" which the organist played over and over and over.

Then, the sin was committed. As I chewed, I choked on the sharp-cornered flake of bread. I choked some more. Then, even more. I grabbed for a tiny glass of grape juice to wash down the bread. And then, I grabbed a second, and a third—long prior to the minister's admonition to drink the

"Blood of Christ." I coughed, and drank more. Jim elbowed me to quit. He made me gasp for air and giggle at the same time. At that point, we were marked. Grape juice spewed forth on my blue frilly dress, on Jim's new gray suit, and on the immaculate, white linen cloth draped on the altar-rail. He began to giggle, too. It was the kind of giggle that had us shaking so hard tears flowed. Mother was aghast. Jim and I wanted to run from the church; but, the only thing we could do was to duck our heads into our hands and quickly follow Mother back to our seats. There, in the Roberts' pew, our barely stifled laughter continued, and even rocked the pew until Jim and I gained enough air to pause and to realize we had "done it" and we were going to "get it." The service ended none too soon. It was just long enough that fear of impending punishment ran rampant in our souls.

At the end of each service, at the large entry door, it was customary for the minister to shake hands with each church-goer, and wish them well for the week. Instead of greeting the minister, Mother quickly retrieved Gary from the basement, and our family left the church by a rear exit to avoid the minister. Once we were all in the car, Father slowly drove the five miles to our home. There was silence—heavy, heavy silence. Then, Father began to chuckle. Then, Mother began to chuckle. Jim and I, the grape-juice-covered perpetrators in the backseat, the ones who had sinned, looked at one another in confusion. Father, with a perfect view of our bread and juice affair, had had to hold in his own laughter as the tragedy unfolded. Mother had just given up and followed Father's "assessment" of the situation.

I must say that, in the coming days, there were serious, extremely serious, instructions regarding proper church behavior. Those severe instructions, however, were always followed by a delightful chuckle of memory. Congregation members who called, and inquired about our vile sin, were told only that the matter was certainly being taken care of. As irreverent as we seemed that ghastly Sunday, Jim and I did return with the family for the next week's service. As usual, we entered the imposing stone church though the front door. We took our seats, two rows from the back, and four places from the left. The leading and portentous members of the church board of directors did more than glance at us that morning. Their looks, their stares, bored into us to see if we were still acting sinfully. I believe that Jim's head-bowed, calm behavior and my demure smile provided assurance to those gentlemen—assurance that we would never again be marked by the grape-juice-sin.

Amen.

Memory is the act of reviewing past things learned and retained. Delicacy
is the art of refined perception and sensitivity. Such defining may appear
as a rather formal way to begin a story about a horseback ride. However,
that ride heightens my own vision in beautiful ways. Memory and Delicacy,
the two words together, engage me once again in a childhood adventure.

Rock Creek Memories and Delicacies

I am twelve-years-old, which may account for my last place in line and for the horse on which I ride—a big black and white fellow who goes by the name of "Dynamite." This name, however, does not reflect his speed. My family— father, mother, brother—riding their respective horses, moves steadily up the mountain path to the head of Rock Creek, a small stream in the southern San Juan Mountains of Colorado. I must kick and urge ol' Dynamite to catch up with the other horses. Too often, he abruptly stops to munch on the fresh, sweet grass. The reins jerk down each time Dynamite halts for this delicacy. I am nearly pulled off the saddle when he does so. Finally, Dynamite shows some interest in ambling up the narrow path between aspen which really do "whisper." I am enthralled that I can ride my own horse. I do not have to share the back of the saddle in which my brother sits. Besides, his saddle always pinches my legs. I do not like miles of pinching. Today, however, I have gained my independence. I ride my own steed.

Dynamite and I mosey on up the path as the aspen turn to pine trees. When we come to a narrow valley, we quietly observe a large herd of elk on a high ridge. They also observe our small family. We have entered their private domain. The elk watch us closely as we ride through the mountain meadow where wild flowers bloom profusely. What delicacy of colors—bright red, deep purple, soft lavender, light blue, intense yellow, and striking white. What delicacy of smells—lung-filling sweet, bittersweet, pungent pine, fir, and spruce. These stately giants now provide deep shadows as we move along paths made of their needles dropped seasons ago. Soon, these trees will begin to give way to shrubs bent low by years of wind and heavy snows.

I take deep breaths of the cool, thin air at this 11,000-foot-high level we have attained on these mountains. It is difficult to contain my excitement when I look out over thousands and thousands of acres of forest. In the distance, the "Four Corners" of Colorado, New Mexico, Utah, and Arizona meet one another. I can "see" much at this altitude. Time runs backward for me. Dynamite and I halt. With inner joy and with my vivid imagination, I watch a tribe of Ute Indians crossing our path as they silently move down into the San Luis Valley with its meandering Rio Grande River where they will camp. I see these ancient people ride spotted ponies with colorful red and yellow blankets, and with decorative leather strands and feathers. Woven baskets on their backs carry their cache of food. I watch them in love and wonder, and wave knowingly to my "friends" as they flow by moving on in this realm of my dream world.

A shout at me brings me back to this day, and Dynamite and I hurry to catch up with the rest of the family. Our trek to reach the headwaters of Rock Creek, now a small four-foot-wide stream at its largest point, has not been solely to observe this beautiful environment. We are in search of the elusive native Brook Trout which inhabit the cold, clear pools of water. We pause, dismount, tether the horses, and remove our hunting equipment—fishing rods. I check my reel, line, and hook. My father has just dug into some soft soil for our bait. I take a worm, quite wiggly, and place it on the hook. I try not to think about this process, only about the wonderful result—catching a trout. I already imagine tasting that special delicacy.

Once prepared, I carefully belly-crawl to within five feet of the little creek. No soldier has ever used elbows as well as I do to reach my goal. I ever-so-slowly extend my fishing rod over the edge of the creek's bank. Then, I let the line, with worm on hook, drop-drop-sink into a small pool of water. Bam! The worm-hook has been hit, the bait has been taken. I gently reel that fish to the bank and slide it onto the grass near me. I want to jump up and yell, "I'm the first. I caught my fish!" But, I don't dare. If I do, I will permanently scare any other fish that my family might catch at their places along the bank. I stifle my adrenaline rush, crawl back to my fishing bag, and tuck my trophy in with fresh, sweet grass. Once more, I "load" my rod and move toward the creek. Once more, I will try to catch a prize.

Each of us in our family of four catches three-to-four trout, and retires to rest against some smooth lichen-covered boulders. There, as we enjoy a late lunch of peanut butter and jelly sandwiches wrapped in wax-paper, potato chips, and icy water in metal canteens, we laugh and compliment ourselves on our "championship" fishing skills. With the caught fish wrapped and secured in our canvass bags, we gather the horses that have been dozing or grazing on the lush, blue-green grass. Then, we adjust the bridles, and cinch-up the saddles in order to begin our return trek. Again, as I ride, I feel the familiar rocking motion as we head down the same path we had earlier negotiated. However, Dynamite now trots, and he and I lead the line of the other family members. He, too, must know that there is a delicacy for him waiting at the end of the path. Our trip back to the truck, horse trailer, and campground takes only a little more than two hours, in contrast to the three hours to reach the head of the creek.

There is, indeed, something special waiting at the bottom of the trail. Even though I once more observe, smell, sense the magnificent trees, the myriad flowers, and the verdant grass that I had enjoyed so much on the trip up the mountain, I am more than anxious to arrive at our base camp. The family wends its way down along Rock Creek through the fir and pine, and finally arrives at our camp's aspen grove. We dismount, and I hurry to hobble the horses so they may graze, and also enjoy some tasty rolled oats we have brought for them. Dynamite is in his glory.

Then comes the reward, the process—what I have anticipated for the past hours of riding. I help to build a fire in a Forest Service grate, remove from the storage pack big yellow onions, Red McClure potatoes, salt, pepper, Crisco, and the *coup de grace*-sweet yellow cornmeal. One enormous, black, cast-iron skillet, placed on the grate to heat from the steadily burning logs, is soon ready for the cornmeal-dusted trout my father has cleaned. In a second cast-iron skillet, the sliced potatoes and onions simmer, spiced only with salt and pepper. I eagerly watch. I hear the crackling of the fire. I hear the sizzling sound of frying food. I hear the scrape of the spatulas turning the potatoes, onions, and fish. The tantalizing aroma is like no other as finally all is ready. Tin plates, warmed on the grate, hold the delicacies. On my fine plate rest delicious potatoes with onions and, of course, the delectable cornmeal-encrusted fried trout. Near the fire, I find a large, flat rock on which I arrange myself for the evening repast. This is truly "dining out."

At first, I restrain myself and take time to closely observe what is before me. Then... then, I have my first bite of trout. That appetizing morsel melts in my mouth. The taste of the trout is soon followed by that of the potatoes and onions cooked to perfection. Icy spring water in tin cups cleanses the palate between bites of food. Too soon, I feel a kind of sadness that the meal is coming to an end. Well, not quite an end, I soon learn. There are more delicacies to follow. Over the low-burning fire, we now simmer, cook, and crisp marshmallows on long, sharpened, green willow sticks. Sticky, very sticky, can only describe the squishy, scrumptious taste.

Dusk surrounds us as we now sit by the fire recalling the adventures of the day. I remember the stunning sights. I feel the motion of horse and saddle. I smell the flowers, grass, and trees. I taste the trout, potatoes, onions, and marshmallows. I sit before the warm, glowing embers. We tell stories. I begin to nod my head sleepily. But, my mind holds so clear the visions of the day. Memory after memory. Delicacy after delicacy.

THE MIDDLE PLACE

Terrorized, horrified, distressed, stunned, paralyzed, and a.Ifrighted
are words that can describe many fear-ftlled incidents. However,
curdled one's blood, made one's blood run cold, put one's heart in
one's mouth, turned one's stomach, scared one's living body stiff, and
jumped out of one's skin are phrases that might more adequately describe
the 4-H cooking event at which I was a young demonstrator.
I didn't succumb completely to the descriptions. But, I could have.

Muffins and Me

"Today... uh, this morning, I... uh, would like to tell you... uh, how to make moist, and light, and delicious 4-H Muffins." The audience of mothers, grandmothers, 4-H club leaders and members held its collective breath as I began the required cooking demonstration as a representative for our Little Daisy 4-H Cooking Club.

"1. Select a large, pretty bowl to mix your ingredients in. 2. Place measuring cups and spoons and the bowl on the table in a neat... uh, orderly way. 3. Open a sack of flour."

There were, of course, other ingredients I spoke of. What they were I don't know. I don't want to know. I don't like muffins. I never liked muffins.

Allow me to elaborate why—why my psyche was irreparably scarred by my acquaintance with muffins. I was nine-years-old, just old enough to have been urged (Read as: forced) to become a member of the Little Daisy 4-H Cooking Club. Now, we eleven girls—yes, all girls in 1953—were supposed to learn how to make various foodstuffs. I don't recall exactly what foodstuffs they were. I just remember the muffins. Our Club leader was a smiling, kindly, well-endowed woman, who lovingly and tenderly encouraged our endeavors. (Read as: "Listen up, you little dummies! If you don't learn to cook, you'll never be able to get married, and you'll never amount to anything!") That subtext of encouragement proved to be true. I never learned to cook, and I never got married. Some people think I didn't amount to anything either. However, I digress.

As the year passed, each Little Daisy Club member developed a skill in cooking one of the foodstuffs which I still cannot recall. I only remember muffins. And, god, did I make muffins. I made a million muffins. Because I made one batch almost correctly, I was chosen for the honor (Read as: dreaded dubious distinction) of giving a public demonstration of my skill.

I had to write a "script" for my demonstration. The words were supposed to go along with my actually showing how to make those stupid muffins. Since my writing skills were ever so much better than my mixing skills, the text for the presentation was rather good. However, as I practiced fixing and mixing, gut-wrenching fear and nausea would overcome me. It became my modus operandi to sit in the bathroom while I rehearsed the words and mimed the demonstrating in case of…. Well, it was just easier to be near the facility. The closer the day of the deed, the more time I spent there. I wanted to die, but I thought I would leave that for the actual day of the demonstration which arrived one sticky, hot, Saturday morning in late August. I got up early, already in panic mode, because I had to make a dozen perfect display muffins. These muffins were to sit on the demonstration table as a shining example of the end of the mixing and baking process. (The event was sort of like a "Julia Child Show." Assemble the stuff, and at the end of the show pull out the finished product from the fake, wall oven.) Between 5:00 a.m. and 8:00 a.m., I prepared at least six-dozen muffins. The very last set made the grade. The dog ate all the other imperfect samples, then, went to the yard to throw up, I guess. I went to the bathroom to do likewise, I guess.

All the various 4-H cooking clubs in the county gathered at 10:00 that morning in the claustrophobic basement of the First Baptist Church. The scents of the various foods made me even more nauseous than I already was. When my mother, and my grandmother, and I entered the room, they smiled at their friends. I grimaced at my friends. All the club leaders were in attendance, as was, dear god, the District 4-H Leader. She was the hostess of the event. She was the queen of daytime demonstrations. She was the director of our little 4-H Heads, Hands, Hearts, and Health.... And, I feared her.

The members of the other clubs displayed their skills first, because they were older, had more experience, and made more interesting foods. Oh,... did I neglect to mention the affair was being held as a contest to select the young women and little girls who would go to the Colorado State Fair to compete in demonstrations there? The District lady shared this tidbit of information just before she introduced each of the club leaders, our dear full-bosomed-one included, and thanked them for all their hard work. I don't think she thanked the club members. I wanted to run from the basement confines. Unfortunately, I was securely held in place by my mother and my grandmother.

Our Little Daisy 4-H Cooking Club was the last on the demonstration agenda, and I was the last member to present the "Favorite 4-H Muffins." Making muffins had an elementary status in the cooking hierarchy, it seemed. When the District Leader called my name at about 12:00, she was clearly tired and bored, as were most of the attendees. I was not tired and bored. I was terrified. Then, something happened to me. I stood up from my sequestered place, flipped back my hair, and marched to the front of the room. I retrieved my box of materials—and the wonderful champion-quality muffins I had made so early that morning. I casually dumped everything, except the muffins, onto the demonstration table. I ever so carefully arranged those golden-brown delights on a red- checked, cloth napkin in a little, wicker basket. There I was, proudly thrusting out my chest—or lack thereof, appearing like the winner I knew I would be.

As I had been taught, I looked up at the audience to begin my demonstration. At that point, my eyes glazed over. The elephants played hopscotch with the butterflies in my stomach. I stood petrified. Miss District Leader half- smiled, and told me to begin. There was a moment of silence— probably two-to-three minutes of moments. Miss District Leader again told me to begin. I took a breath. No words. Miss District Leader cleared her throat. I cleared mine. "My name is…." I muttered something unintelligible. That was followed by: "Today… uh, this morning, I… uh, would like…." Well, you remember the beginning of this story. Once I got to the opening of the sack of flour, disaster loomed on the horizon of that church basement wall. I began to speak rapidly. Indy-500 formula cars could not have matched my speed that day. In addition, my actions did not match the words I had so carefully written and memorized. I was still speaking, for the third time, about how to place the utensils on the work table as I began to put the flour into the measuring cup. And, boy, did I put flour into that measuring cup. I put in one spoonful, and another, and another, and another. To be sure that I had enough, I took the spoon and packed that flour again and again. Then, I smacked it once more just to be sure the cup was full. Note: Muffins are to be light and fluffy and airy. To help them achieve that status, the flour is sifted and ever so gently spooned into the measuring cup, and thence, into the mixing bowl.

I do not recall much after that point in my demonstration. There was some sort of audience response. It was not applause. It sounded more like birds twittering—chuckling actually. From somewhere, I heard a whiny, nasally sort of voice. "Thank you, young lady. That was a very, ah... interesting demonstration." I stared at her like the proverbial deer caught in headlights. Then came the critique. "Young lady, are you aware of what you have just done?" I closed my eyes. My chin dropped to my chest. She continued, "Young lady, are you aware that if you actually baked the mixture you put together, you would have something even a baseball bat could not break?" My knees felt as if they were collapsing. I grasped the edge of the table for balance. The mistress of misery was on a roll. "Furthermore, you could not possibly have made these sample muffins. You have just demonstrated that you do not know how to do so." She smirked at me. She smiled at the audience. She sweetly thanked them for coming. Then, she happily reminded the attendees that the winners of the demonstrations would be announced within a week.

As the mothers and daughters began to leave, I just stood there for a long five minutes, with an inner-smile forming. I surmised that traveling to the State Fair was not in my future. I could breathe again. A lovely sense of relief began to envelop me. I had survived the demonstration torture chamber. Of course, I still had to face the judgment of our formidable leader... and my formidable mother... and my formidable grandmother. Their looks needed no words to be interpreted.

Soon after that inglorious day in August, I left the Little Daisy 4-H Cooking Club forever, and looked elsewhere for my Head, Hands, Heart, and Health, especially the last. I saw the light, so to speak, and found far more pleasant territory around the corrals and in the meadows of our ranch. I was proud. I worked hard. I became an immensely happy member—of the Windy Peak 4-H Livestock Club.

Post Script: You may be pleased to learn that my handsome, award-winning, champion-of-the-show, Hereford steer ate only scrumptious rolled-oats and succulent hay. He never did eat a muffin.

In my young life, I fought an inner-battle to satisfy a need to be acknowledged, to be noticed, to be more than non-object. For a brief time, however, the battle eased and I was able to see that elusive need met through concern and care and, dare I say, love.

Wanting to Exist

Warm, June days signaled completion of the fifth grade and the coming of my eleventh birthday. As summer moved toward July, I lacked energy, experienced aches and pains, and, then, developed a fever that became worse each day. I tried to say nothing about how I felt. I knew I always had to be strong, to do my chores, to be OK… because I feared disapproval from both parents. Particularly, I feared that she, my step-mother, would speak to me in anger, or not speak to me at all. The latter meant I simply did not exist.

However, the physical symptoms soon became too obvious, too severe, by the time for my special day. I needed medical help. Reluctantly, my parents agreed. My step-mother, noting that it was a burden, took me to see a physician in northern New Mexico, about a two-hour drive from our home in southern Colorado. I immediately liked Dr. Michael, or "Dr. M." as I came to call him. This husky, burly, French-Canadian with bright, animated, silver-blue eyes, captivated my curiosity. Aware of my quiet interest, he took time to tell me about his work, about leaving the eastern environs of Johns Hopkins University, and about establishing his internal medicine practice in the dry, desert-like, southwest climate. He had chosen New Mexico as a place to care for his own health, a menacing asthma condition.

Within a few hours of our morning appointment, my illness had a name. It posed a major health problem for me. I had an advanced case of rheumatic fever. That afternoon, the doctor ordered that I be hospitalized. I remained so for more than two months. At the time of the decision, and during the days that followed, my step-mother expressed only displeasure with the doctor's directives. She resented the entire process. Even though I tried to get her to understand I would rather be with her, she rejected me and anything I said. It was as if I had no value. "You just stay here, then. I have to get home to do all the work now." That day, she left me in a town unknown to me, in a hospital unknown to me, in the company of people unknown to me.

With significant concern that I be properly cared for, that days became a wonder-filled "known." Sensing my anxiety and my fear, the nurses and staff members embraced me with care, gentleness, and a kind of love— secure, safe, consistent. "Dr. M." took it upon himself to teach me Scrabble. "Go ahead. I dare you to see how you can gain points with the letter Q." He created an ongoing game we played when he made rounds each morning and evening. When medical affairs began to fascinate me, that interest was openly encouraged. My "hospital friends" brought health magazines, histories of medicine, and biographies of famous physicians, nurses, researchers, all chosen to be read to me and by me.

"Come on, missy. Let's get moving." Those words were called out on numerous afternoons. The tall, usually stern, head surgical nurse, Tina, would openly laugh as she bent down and pushed me along in my wheelchair. "Today, we see Operating Suite # 1, and all of its special instruments. I think you'll like them." As fascinated as I was, I surmised the real purpose of her endeavors was to finally wend our way to the hospital kitchen. There, she and a delightfully funny cook, Marta, made the most incredibly delicious egg-nog concoctions for me. My desire for food was poor because of the illness; but, as a favor to both, I would slowly drink the tall, full glasses of thick, creamy liquid. "Special drink vill help you be gut. You soon be strong, mein Liebchen," Marta would always say in her soft German accent.

Despite the obvious absence of my mother and father, and despite the aches and pains in my joints, indeed throughout my whole body, the weeks in the hospital provided moments of sheer joy. I fell in love with the "love" demonstrated by my doctor and all the people at that hospital. In a rather odd sort of way, being ill made me feel well—except on the rare Saturdays when my step-mother drove down from Colorado. Disgusted that I was too slow in recovering, she would repeatedly remark, "I don't see any reason why you can't be at home. There's plenty of work to be done there."

My time in the hospital came to an unexpected, abrupt end one early morning, an end demanded by her. This sudden departure was not a happy-farewell-occasion. She forced me to leave behind all the books and gifts from the staff. Other unimportant items brought from home were quickly placed in brown paper bags. I had no way to go to each friend to say thank you or even good-bye. All that I had known and loved for weeks was gone as the last bits of time rushed by. I could feel only a tremendous sense of loss, of emptiness, of an encroaching void.

With a firm attitude and awareness of my special needs, that wonderful, loving physician gave explicit instructions about medications and exercise. The final directive was for her to keep me at home during the first semester of sixth grade. He believed that I was more than capable of keeping up with my subjects by reading and completing school work at home at my own pace—and by resting and resting.

My step-mother always resisted anyone giving her orders. She especially detested those given by "my doctor- friend." She openly fought the doctor's orders. And, she strongly criticized the value of any time I spent on my schoolwork. When I researched and wrote a story about the Paricutin volcano in Mexico, and carefully drew pictures of the massive mountain, she simply told me that what I was doing was wasted effort. "You're really not that sick anymore. It's time you do some real work around here. Just stop your day-dreaming, and your talk about that hospital. I don't want to hear another word about it." She did not.

In my private moments, I retreated into my remembrance-world where I could envision all that had occurred in New Mexico and at home. Otherwise, I tried to follow her forceful expectations to work. The indoor tasks of washing dishes, making beds, sweeping floors, and the outdoor tasks of gathering the eggs, feeding the chickens, took their toll. The pain I still felt was exhausting. Yet, I said nothing. I did those chores. I did them as instructed. And, I did them with fear—fear that she would punish me physically and emotionally.

Although I was still quite weak and unsteady, I attempted other tasks that went far beyond what she ordered. I chose to crawl on my hands and knees on the grass to dig up dandelions. I chose to drag alfalfa bales to feed the sheep. I chose to scoop ammonia-smelling, acrid droppings from chicken roosts. I chose to perform the worst possible tasks. She never commented on them.

Why did I try, again and again? Because... because, I needed to. I wanted to. I thought and hoped that if I could do them, she would be pleased with me, perhaps would love me. Most of all, I hoped she would speak to me— with thanks or even anger—to acknowledge me somehow. If or when that happened, I knew that I finally would exist to her. I wanted to exist.

An old juniper tree grew for years and years in the northwest corner of our expansive lawn. That tree bore firm steel-blue-gray berries every year, and, as a child, I made distinctly negative comments about their repulsive odor. Only later, as a young adult, did I learn those same berries formed the basis for gin. Even with that knowledge, I still made negative comments about the odor —and the taste. Then, I acquired a new vision when I met a drink of the unusual product—Hendrick's Gin. Within it, coriander, citrus peel, rose petal, and cucumber gave the juniper-berry concoction a curious, marvelous taste. Now, I sip my new-found gin with tonic, or sip my new-found friend as martini. Now, I no longer despise juniper trees.

It Is Not For Everybody

Hendrick's Gin—Grey Goose or Three Olive Vodka—Balvenie or Glenfiddich or Speyside Scotch, 18-year-old, please. These varieties stand firmly in the forefront of my repertoire of alcoholic preferences. Indeed, a nice Italo Cescon Pinot Grigio, or even an Irish Bennington Ale have touched my palate. I do love a juniper, wheat, barley, or grape elixir on special occasions. A certain wicked delight descends when the befuddled bartender has never heard of, or does not have my request on hand. So, I take a deep breath and exhale in an oh-so-disappointed-manner, "Well... I suppose that Bombay Sapphire will have to do."

"A Personal Accounting"

I must make it perfectly clear that I did not consume any alcohol until my junior year in college. As an eighteen- year-old, I was legally permitted to drink "3.2 beer" in the state of Colorado. Friends from eastern states often thought they could consume large quantities of 3.2 % beer, because they were used to efficiently handling 6% beer. It took only one, maybe two, mugs for them to understand the effect of the San Luis Valley's 7,652-foot-altitude on alcoholic intake.

As I recall, there were only two nefarious occasions when strong spirits crossed my lips. At one off-campus gathering, I sampled my first, and last, rum and Coca-Cola. The sickish-sweetness of that combination made me move rapidly to plates of salty crackers and cheese. I still think the drink ghastly, gagging reflex, along with a sense of horror that anyone could find pleasure in burned, rotten, rubber tires. The swig was whiskey—the worst, cheapest, vilest, half-pint, partially-hidden-in-a-rolled-down-paper-bag-kind-of-whiskey. Many years passed before I learned of the "real" taste and texture of a "fine" scotch drink with a cube or two of ice.

No beautiful, tasteful, restaurant served as the setting for my education occasion in the art of the drink. Friend Mo and I ventured to Estes Park, Colorado, for the sizeable, yearly Scottish-Irish Festival. On the grounds were tents for each of the clans, tents for purchasing apparel, jewelry, and assorted memorabilia, and tents for food vendors offering a wide array of Celtic foodstuffs. As we perused the contents of the tents, one set stood out, not only because of the colorful kilts the proprietors wore, but also because of the large, and intriguing, banners displaying names of Scottish drinks. I was reluctant to go in, but Mo insisted. "Look, it can't hurt to learn about their craft of brewing." "I don't know. We've got to get to the parade of the clans." "Good grief, it's just 10:30. Let's at least look over the items."

When we entered the tent, the gentlemen quickly informed us that no bottles of brew could be purchased. However, for a mere dollar we could drink samples of the products. The rather good-looking "server" offered us gin and scotch—the first to Mo, the latter to me. "Mo, I really don't want to sample this stuff." "M'lady," the fellow interrupted and addressed Mo with a slight bow. "May I offer you our Hendrick's Gin with a tidge of tonic." "Well, I'm not much of a gin-person." "Oh, you will be soon." he noted, as he placed a slice of cucumber on the rim of her glass. "You must, my dear, use cucumber. Lemon or lime slices will demolish the herb, rose hips, and, of course, the light juniper flavor." Mo was enchanted enough by his gracious manner—and brogue—to succumb to sipping, then drinking the gin. That glass led to two more samples. "Oh, my goodness, you've got to try this." "Ah, no, ma'am." remarked a burly fellow with a silver-gray beard which complemented my own graying locks. "This lady has to allow her palate the taste of Glenfiddich with a few ice cubes to chill it." I smiled cordially. "I'd rather not. Thank you, though." Visions of burning rubber tires came to mind. I thought it best to leave.

The gentleman, however, was persistent, as he blocked my exit. "Ah, ma'am, don't dismiss this drink so quickly. Here, do try a sip." Knowing the taste would be god-awful, I hesitantly accepted the glass, and slowly raised it to my lips. There was no burning smell. Then, came a smooth— highly polished smooth—taste of an 18-year-old wonder of a drink. Mo interrupted my reverie. "Here, try this Hendrick's. It's more than delightful." She urged me to take a sip. "No way. I've finally found my drink of choice." To demonstrate, I tried a couple more samples of my choice.

With much reluctance, Mo and I left, sort of drifted away from the intriguing tent. We feared we would become too attached to its contents with one more sip to entice us. Also, we'd had little breakfast, so on we carefully moved to a food vendor's tent for some breakfast items, including Scottish eggs. It was a needed bit of sustenance to soak up some of our drinking experiment. We finally did make our way to the parade grounds to listen to and watch with awe the mass entrance of all the clans with bagpipes, accompanied by the Continental Fife and Drum Corps, and the U.S. Marine Corps Band. When a lone piper began "Amazing Grace," and was gradually joined by each of the groups, tears came. Mo and I were amazed in our own way. "We've found the best of festivals, the best of foods, and, well... the best of drinks for imbibing memories."

"Moravian Manners"

Many individuals, some close acquaintances, have inquired on numerous occasions if any form of alcohol was ever present, at any time, in any Roberts home. "Roberts" included my great-grandfather, my grandfather, and my father. The answer was always a firm "No." I question that word. "Yes" is more accurate. There was rubbing alcohol, first-aid alcohol, cough-syrup alcohol, and vanilla-extract alcohol. However, it may be unfair to include the last, since it was used as a part of food preparation. I do, though, remember a time when "rum balls" were brought into our abode by a Christmas-time guest.

In my early years, I questioned why there was such a limit on alcohol in our activities—at home and anywhere else I could think of. Answer? First word: Grandfather. Second word: Grandfather. As a believer in old Methodist directives, that fine gentleman had principles. Avoiding alcohol consumption was among the top of his many strongly-held precepts. Now, it must be said that Grandfather was not a Carrie Nation, axe-wielding, barrel-breaking teetotaler. What he said and did about alcohol was subdued, befitting the calm demeanor of his heritage as the son of a Welsh immigrant farmer. His particular ancestors certainly did not adhere to the better-known lifestyles of Dylan Thomas and Richard Burton.

There was no stopping for lunch or dinner at any restaurant or other establishment displaying a "Coors" or "Pabst" neon sign in its window. He never uttered a negative comment; he just calmly drove on by the place. Grandfather's preferences almost seemed genetic, because my father felt and acted in a similar fashion regarding alcoholic beverages, until... until the Coors Beer Distilling Company ventured into the San Luis Valley.

The Golden, Colorado, firm had long been known for its light-colored concoction brewed with "pure Rocky Mountain spring water." In the mid-1950s, Coors' representatives came to the Valley and assessed the quality of barley that was raised there for cattle feed. These men approached a number of farmers whose fields were exceptional in quality. That meant that few, if any, herbicides or pesticides were ever applied to the plants. And, the barley was of exceptional, golden color throughout the fields. My father was one of those growers. The Coors Company offered him the opportunity to plant, grow, and harvest a special kind of barley—Moravian. Coors would provide the barley seed, my father would grow and harvest the grain, and the brewing company would purchase the beautiful barley to use in its remarkable brewing process. Dollar signs floated onto many a contract for a number of farmers who made such arrangements with Coors. The family knew that if our father accepted the Coors offer, we would be exceedingly comfortable with the added income from the sales of the Moravian barley.

However, those dollar signs quickly flew away when Grandfather heard of the Coors interest, and of the impending deal, and of the contract that was to be signed one fall day. A slight glitch in the proceedings occurred. Though retired, Grandfather still owned many of the acres of land on which the Moravian barley would be grown. He was not pleased when he learned of the upcoming monetary arrangement, but had said little about his concerns. Grandfather simply arrived from town the day the contract between my father and Coors was to have been negotiated. The representatives from Coors stood solemnly and observed the scene. With a firm, though graceful, sense of purpose, Grandfather stepped from his silver-hued Oldsmobile-98, and strolled over to my father and the Coors men. No discussion occurred among the three parties. His disarming smile seemed a positive indicator regarding the event to come. However, as dispassionately as possible, Grandfather stated, "Sirs, no beer barley will ever be grown on this land." He smiled cordially to the dropped-jaw representatives, courteously tipped his hat, turned away, and again with a sense of purpose, walked to his car, got in, and drove back to his home in town. Nothing more needed to be said.

"It's All in the Name"

"Those red and white Herefords made for a beautiful scene on our lush, green meadows." Dad remarked during one of my Christmas breaks when I visited my parents, now retired and residing for the winter in Mesa, Arizona. "Yes, Dad, but the white wool of the Columbias was also striking against the dark-green alfalfa fields." "Remember how doggone mean those cows could be if you got between one and her calf." "Well, the ewes seemed to select a few of their own to watch their lambs run up and down the ditch-banks playing stop-and-go games." "What is this... a competition about who's better—Herefords or Columbias?" "Hey, definitely not by me. You're the one who raised the grass and alfalfa, the cattle and the sheep." Dad thought a minute and responded. "Well... as I recall, you had your own little herd of sheep that gave you a college education. By the way, what was your first ewe's name? Thought it seemed an odd choice." Now it was my turn to consider a thought. "Dad, there's a whole story about that ewe and her name. I think you're old enough now to hear it."

"I'm sure you remember the cold, late February days, when all those pregnant ewes gave birth to the little ones. You said that getting twin lambs or even healthy triplets, was good, as long as the mother had enough milk and could care for them." "Sure... I knew that way there'd be more lambs to replenish the herd and to sell in June. I know I'm 85, but I'll never forget each year when we shipped the fat lambs to Denver to Producers' Livestock Marketing Association." "Yes, and precisely at noon each day, Denver's KOA radio announcer listed whose lambs had arrived." "I know... I made you all sit still and listen to the report to hear that the Roberts' lambs from Monte Vista got the highest price for that day." "One lamb never made it to Denver one year, Dad. That little ewe became the head of my own herd of sheep.... And, so on the story goes."

"One icy February morning—I think it was in 1954 —you brought a lamb to your workroom that housed the big, coal furnace, the hot water tanks, and the pumps which took water to the corrals." He nodded. "You don't think I'd ever forget the warmth that place provided, do you." "No, I don't. But on that day you told mother and me that poor, scraggly, infant lamb was about to die. You thought maybe we could save it, or at least give it a try. Then you went back to the sheep sheds."

"So, mother and I first wrapped the little thing in warm burlap towels, rubbing it and rubbing it, to dry it and get it warm. Then, we tried to get it to suckle warm milk from a rubber-nippled bottle. But, it just lay there with its mouth becoming colder and colder. You always said that was a sure sign of dying. There was no way I wanted that lamb to die. I ran to the kitchen to make some really strong hot tea. I knew that sometimes tea helped warm an animal's insides enough to help it hang on and live. But the tea we tried to get her to drink didn't help. I just knew there was nothing more we could do. Suddenly, mother said to hold her close and keep her warm for a second. Then, she went to that tall, wooden cabinet which held all the medicines, ointments, bag-balm, and such for the horses, cattle, and sheep. She stood on a chair, reached behind some old bottles on the top shelf, and retrieved an even older-looking one. She sighed thinking that this was our last hope. I sort of gasped and mumbled something like, "But, it's... how did it... ?" She told me to be quiet, saying that the bottle belonged to an old foreman who was long gone. She had never thrown it away. It was always where he left it." That little lamb, rejected by its mother, was about to take its last breath.

I held open its cold mouth, and Mom forced in a small swig of the elixir from the previously-hidden, half-pint of Four Roses Whiskey. I knew she was dying, and tears welled-up in my eyes. But, I guess strange things do happen. The lamb swallowed that little sip, then another. She paused a second, opened her eyes—bright and clear. Within one minute—and I mean one minute— that lamb was standing up on four, steady legs. She shook her knobby wool coat, looked at Mom, and looked at me. Then, she began to bleat, not in a weak, whimpering way, but with a strong sound that demanded milk. She took that rubber nipple and suckled the entire bottle of milk until her shallow, caved-in sides looked like little round balloons. When she finished, she rubbed her fuzzy head against my hand, curled up in warm blankets on my lap, and found rest in her sleep."

"In a whisper, I asked if we could keep her. I knew that the mother ewe would never accept her now with all the strange odors on her—especially that Four Roses smell. I really wondered what would happen to her. As my tears welled up once more, I began to babble about the lamb being all mine, that I'd take good care of her, that she'd have to have a name. I thought a moment, then came up with Poor Four Rosie. There was a pause, then mother chuckled, saying that it was much too big for such a little lamb, even though it had saved the lamb's life. She emphasized that the family doesn't touch that alcohol stuff, and heaven forbid what your dad might say. I held the lamb closer, and thought some more. Then I suggested that we just call her... Soda Pop. After all, we did drink that. Thus, how we named her became our long-held little secret."

"And so, Soda Pop became my lamb, Dad. You remember, I bottle fed her each day before and after school. When she was old enough, she munched on sprigs of sweet clover and alfalfa. Sometimes I sneaked her some rolled- oats. She grew and grew. Her coat was beautiful, thick, white wool. Even the crimp of the inner wool was tight and clean and perfect. That ewe lamb stood out from all the other orphan lambs we raised, and the ones you raised, too, Dad. When the big herd's spring lambs were ready to be sold, I feared saying goodbye to her. But, do you also remember that I came up with a solution—a rather simple one, actually. Soda Pop was a ewe lamb. I would keep her, raise her, eventually breed her to one of your

Columbia bucks, and help Soda Pop raise her own lambs—twins, I hoped. So, I claimed her to be always mine. Once she had grown up, her mature male lambs were sold just as those in your herd were, Dad. As you recall, in the years that followed, Soda Pop had more and more lambs. Some I sold, others I kept. My little herd expanded, and my education expanded. All thanks to Soda Pop... and that miracle elixir."

In one way, as I view this accounting, Soda Pop did provide the resources, the money for my education. In another way, an exceedingly special way, the story is Soda Pop's. As tiny and weak as she was, hope made that lamb a survivor, not a dying orphan, and I see ties to my own life. It was my hope that day that she would live, as I held her ever so close. It was her hope that day to live, as she tasted a bit of her "rosie" future.

Truth and dedication and love are hallmarks of long-standing
relationships—of simple, beautiful friendships we see forever.

Sugar and Secrets

As children, we gather to us fellow school-mates as fast friends. As young adults, we form more fond, solid relationships. As part of an older generation, we also discover those who become especially dear to us. Some of these individuals, a select few, remain ever-so-strongly with us throughout a lifetime. And, when one departs from our life, a portion of us passes also. I felt a profound absence when I lost my distinctive, unconventional friend some years ago. His life and mine were inextricably bound for years.

That friend entered my life on a not-so-ordinary occasion, and came to satisfy the need a young girl had for companionship and unconditional love. One might say, I found in him truth and love and dedication which never faltered throughout his life. Our association began rather early in my teen years—actually the precise day I became a teen-ager.

My thirteenth birthday dawned with doing the usual chores and fulfilling other morning obligations on our ranch. As a treat, I got to spend the day in town with my Grammy Black. We had peanut butter and raspberry jelly sandwiches, and date-stuffed cookies for lunch. We sat in her flower-filled, grassy yard, and played seemingly endless games of Chinese Checkers, most of which she skillfully won. In late afternoon, we returned to the ranch for a dinner of fried chicken and mashed potatoes covered with smooth, white gravy. All those crunchy drumsticks and thighs were superseded in taste by an angel-food-cake decorated in bright, red rose frosting and pink candles. All of this was accompanied with fresh-picked, garden strawberries on top of home-made vanilla ice-cream.

Brightly colored paper and ribbons secured the gifts for the day. I was firmly directed by everyone—Grammy Black, Grandmother and Grandfather Roberts, and my mother and father—that these enticements could not be touched until all the dessert was finished, and the dishes cleared from the table. Weeks earlier I had cautiously put in a request for an animal I could raise as my own. And, I seriously noted that I didn't desire a calf or a lamb.

I had already raised them in 4-H projects. The cards and gifts I opened gave no indication of satisfying that request. Pajamas, blouses, and shoes were quite pretty. But, overall none were too exciting. Three books to add to my favorite "Black Stallion" series seemed as close as I was going to get to my own animal. But, I really did appreciate the gifts because of who gave them to me. Of course, there were delightful cards that accompanied the gifts. A few even had surprise birthday-money in them. However, there was one card saved until all the presents had been opened. When it was handed to me, I slowly examined it, then opened the envelope, and discovered only a folded sheet of paper inside.

This mystery paper contained a series of directions which I was to follow—12 steps through the dining room, 7 steps across the kitchen, 10 steps to the back porch door, 30 steps to the apple orchard. There were more and more steps which finally led me to the door of a two-story white building. I was to open the door and to walk east 50 steps and turn right.... There the directions ended.

So, I did as instructed, and made all the correct steps and turns. The last building, I figured, was our big white barn, and the 50 steps took me down the alley-way to the end stall. Then, just as I turned right, I was greeted by the very loud braying of a very small donkey sporting a huge red satin bow attached to an oversized halter. Here was my secret gift. I rushed to hug the little guy, and he laid his head on my shoulder and made soft crying sounds. This out- of-the-ordinary gift was my very own friend-to-be.

That donkey and I became instant buddies. I named him "Skeeter" because his little nips for attention were more like mosquito bites. Skeeter was grayish-tan in color, with a dark brown cross along his neck, back, and shoulders. He had tall, shaggy, brown-tipped ears, a soft, velvety nose and mouth, and eyes that were deep pools of brown. To me, he was cute, beautiful, and strikingly handsome, all at the same time. When he first arrived, Skeeter was still young enough to want to drink cow's milk from a small pot. Then, that soft nose and mouth would be covered with an old-man white beard and mustache. I think he knew I found that entertaining as he tried to wipe the excess milk on my shirt. In addition to his usual fare of grass, that donkey enjoyed generous portions of sweet-smelling rolled-oats. But, what the young fellow truly relished were slices of white bread covered with a thick mixture of homemade butter and white sugar. This last delicacy remained his favorite throughout his life.

That first summer, Skeeter followed me everywhere. In the grassy yard, I would lie down—Skeeter would lie down. I'd raise my head—Skeeter would raise his. We spent hours together. I would sit against a tree to read a book, and he would kneel down to place his head on my lap. As I turned the pages, he seemed to be listening closely to the sounds of the words. As the only girl in a family with three children, I had longed for someone in whom I could confide. Skeeter satisfied that desire. I could tell him of my dreams and aspirations, and he always responded with soft nudges and contented sounds of "m-m-m."

That donkey freely roamed and grazed in the yard and orchard. As a quite intelligent character, he quickly learned how to open almost any kind of gate, especially the one to the rolled-oats bin. One evening, as I helped to prepare dinner, I glanced into the dining room. Standing at the head of the table was Skeeter, who immediately let out a braying "Hello." He had cleverly opened the porch door by grasping the round doorknob with his teeth, turning it, and pulling the door open... and in he had trotted. Skeeter did not wander so freely after that.

That donkey never wore a saddle or carried a pack load. When he became strong enough as he matured, I would put a halter on him, and slip onto his back. However, if I urged him to go in one direction, he usually chose to go exactly where he wished, or plant his four hooves firmly and not go at all. He constantly entertained with his antics, such as trying to herd the milk cows. Skeeter preferred their passive company in contrast to the biting and kicking of the larger horses. For his endeavors, that little fellow always got lots of rolled-oats, along with the special butter and sugar mixture on a thick slice of bread.

Through my school years, Skeeter was there as a steadfast friend to whom I confided my "secrets" about my life. When I went off to college, I missed my confidante terribly, and even more when I left to teach at a university in Ohio. However, his unfaltering, unconditional love was always there in my life—he never forgot me. When I returned home to Colorado for visits, I'd go to the pasture, call out Skeeter's name, and he would come running, braying all the way. I would hug him, and he would place his big head gently on my shoulder. I'd scratch and rub his face, and whisper "sweet nothings" into those beautiful, tall, shaggy ears. He never failed me.

In the end, I was home the day my friend of twenty-two years died with his head in my lap, as I shared my last "goodbye." When he was buried in his favorite blanket, I placed a box of sugar cubes beside him—for his final journey.

Many years have passed since I took that "birthday walk" and found my true, dear friend. I can still feel Skeeter's head on my shoulder and the touch of his shaggy ears and see the love in those deep brown eyes. Ah-h, the secrets he kept for me. I know one day my friend will come running and braying to me—and Skeeter and I shall again share sugar and secrets.

For a brief time, the child held beautiful glimpses of two exceptional
people. Now, they remain forever a cherished memory.

They Were Given To Love

She was round, buxom, and given to lively laughter.

He was tall, lean, and given to conservative frowns.

She and he, Pearl and Paul, were my grandparents—two special people for a short, too short, a time. There are memories of a day when Grandmother Roberts held me ever so close and whispered, "Hush, child, hush." I was four-years-old. I had lost my mommy. Grandmother's warmth gave me my only solace during that horrible, black time.

Several years passed. My father chose to marry again. I was almost six. The first months of my role as step- daughter were uncomfortable. Days sometimes turned rocky, and were often less than amicable. Grandfather and Grandmother seemed to stop by our ranch at just the right time to take me for a car ride. Their caring showed no limitations. They took me on special picnics up into the nearby mountains, and let me wade and play in the chilly waters of little Rock Creek. They took me across the San Luis Valley to Mineral Hot Springs to paddle in the warm waters of the huge old swimming pool. They took me on shopping sprees to Montgomery Ward Department Store. I was delighted by the way Grandfather called the large store "Monkey Ward." It had every kind of clothing, tools, furniture, and toys. I always wished there were monkeys in it, too.

All these times together with Grandmother and Grandfather, though exciting for me, brought on simmering anger and a short temper from my step-mother. When I returned from each outing, she displayed her ire. She wanted me at home to do work, even though I always completed my chores. I had not yet learned the full meaning of the words "threat" and "jealousy." But, something akin to those words brought bad feelings deep inside me, as I saw the person I had to call "Mommy" interact with Grandmother and Grandfather.

Not to be deterred, those two wonderful people kept close contact with me. My elementary school was only two blocks from their home on quiet, tree-lined, Dennis street. Memories come—of scrumptious lunches of fried, pink salmon patties, with corn-on-the-cob, and icy milk. Memories come— of Grandfather making me giggle as he teased me in his gargling-sounding Welsh words. Memories come—of Grandmother insisting that I take a nap covered by her bright yellow, red, and blue crocheted afghan on a day-bed in her darkened study.

Being with the two of them was much like an education lesson. Grandfather would test my "numbers" skills, as he put it. Grandmother focused on my use of correct grammar, and taught me when to say "Please" and "Thank You." He and she taught me to always stand graciously when an adult entered the room. These lessons have never been forgotten. I smile in memory.

Every summer, Grandmother and Grandfather offered the *piece de resistance,* as they called it. One beautiful day in July, I would pack blue jeans, red plaid shirts, sturdy brown shoes, toothpaste and toothbrush, plus yellow flannel pajamas. With my little suitcase, I anxiously awaited the arrival of the blue-gray Oldsmoblie-98 towing a shiny, silver Airstream trailer. And, then, I left behind times of confusion when I feared the anger, feared the hurt, feared the non-acknowledgement of even being a person. I filled the backseat of the Olds with almost uncontrollable wiggling and giggling as Grandfather headed our entourage into the San Juan Mountains on old Colorado Highway-160. More excitement reigned when we turned off onto a dirt road that led to the campgrounds alongside Beaver Creek. The icy water, which eventually met the Rio Grande River, flowed by trees, bushes, and rocks making pools and eddies designed, of course, for dipping my bare feet.

Every year of those wonderful summer seasons, Grandfather parked the Airstream by graceful willow bushes, sweet-smelling sagebrush, and tall, hovering pine and fir trees. On our arrival, I shot out of the car like a wild horse from a corral gate. For two glorious weeks, I chased, waded, and galloped my way around the campground territory. There was a large, smooth, steel-gray rock close to the bank of Beaver Creek that looked rather like a swept-wing aircraft. Each day I "flew" that plane-rock down the river and into high space. I found large, pine logs which had fallen across Beaver Creek. Walking on them challenged my minimal gymnastic skills, and was, frankly, a little dangerous. But, always nearby, knitting at a picnic table or collecting twigs and branches for our nightly campfire, were Grandmother and Grandfather, ever watchful, never quite interfering.

Beautiful moments occurred when Grandmother and I ventured forth in search of the elusive gooseberry. She and I would leave early in the morning, frost still on the grass, in search of our "prey." With great glee, I would spot a bush with the pale, green berries ready for picking. My first time, I began grabbing at the branches until Grandmother grasped my hands, held them gently, and showed me how to select the ripe berries one-by-one. With a pail filled with four-to-five cups of sour, really sour, gooseberries, Grandmother and I returned triumphant to carefully wash and prepare the berries for a luscious pie. Sugar, lots of sugar, was needed to make the pie truly a taste treat. The smell of the warm, baked pie did not escape attention. At dinner, Grandfather did the unorthodox act of rapping knife and fork on the dining table demanding "pie-pie-gooseberry pie." The pie was sweet. The pie was tart. Grandmother earned much praise, but made certain I received credit for the hours of picking and cleaning the berries. Such acknowledgement was to be rare throughout my life at home. I treasured the credit this gentle, caring person gave to me on that special night on Beaver Creek.

Grandfather and I had our own little adventures. He had a natural skill with his fishing pole, using flitting lures, sharp-pronged hooks, bright red fish eggs, or squiggly worms to snatch Rainbow Trout from one of the quiet pools of water along the edge of the stream. Grandfather even taught me how to construct a "wilderness" fishing pole from a sapling branch, a long string, and a hook bent from a safety pin. Even though I never caught a fish, the anticipation was well worth the endeavor. Fortunately, Grandfather's skill provided enough fish to eat for an evening meal. At those times, the cleaned trout were dusted in yellow cornmeal, and fried in a sizzling hot, black cast-iron skillet placed on a large grate over the campfire. Grandfather prided himself with his cooking acumen, and took over chef duties in his formal, long, monogrammed, white apron. We all laughed and laughed, but were definitely sure his attention to the work made the trout an extra delectable and delightful meal of fine dining.

Every year, Grandfather took me on a jaunt to find and select just the right seven-inch piece of a green-willow branch. He notched the twig for a mouthpiece, tapped round and round the small stick with the handle of his ever- ready pocket knife. With the tapping, the sticky bark was released from the inner wood. Carefully, he carved the finger holes. Then, he slid the bark back on. The result was my very own whistle with which I tootled away chipmunks, and rabbits, and Blue Jays. I also tootled at two-legged, not-so-wild life. Grandmother always worried about my offending other campers, as I whistled among the bushes and trees along the campground's shaded trails. However, I was the envy of other young campers along Beaver Creek, who followed me as if I was the Pied Piper of the Woods.

Each day of unforgettable events had to come to an end after sticky marshmallow, chocolate, and graham cracker s'mores were made and eaten before the embers of our nightly fire. Licked, then scrubbed hands, fingers, and face signaled bedtime. Our campsite in the mountains was at 8,600 feet in altitude. Even in our Airstream trailer, the chilly July night air dictated sleep in flannel PJs. Once attired, that warm-hearted Grandmother tucked me in under blankets and turned down the gaslights. Then began my last treat of the day. Grandmother sat beside me, and in the soft glow of the lantern read stories. My favorite, which she read again and again, summer after summer, was "Lightfoot the Deer." Each evening, I followed the deer's path until sleep and dreams took over my trek after Lightfoot, the smartest deer in the forest. The last kiss from Grandmother sent me into my dream-imagination world.

I loved Grandmother and Grandfather as they loved me. He would grab me and tickle me in the ribs until I begged him to stop. As I stood before him, he always whispered that I could be anything I wanted to be as I grew up. Then, he would knuckle-rub my head, and would urge me to go to Grandmother. I would quickly run to her for "our" time. She and

I would walk down a grassy, flowered path of blue Colorado Columbines, then sit at a picnic table and feed crackers to raucous Blue Jays, and chat about my future. Grandmother would gently reach around my six-seven-eight-year-old self and draw me close to her with an ever dear moment of sheer love.

Our Beaver Creek sojourns came to an end in a tragic way. I was nine-years-old when that beautiful, gracious lady—and she was a lady—died from injuries sustained in a ghastly car accident on an icy December day. Even in her torn, broken state in that hospital bed, she spoke of love for me.

Grandfather survived the horrible crash, but was in a coma-like state for three long months. He never quite recovered physically or emotionally from his ordeal. However, one thing was always apparent—his love for me.

I shall never forget them.

She was round, buxom, and given to lively laughter. He was tall, lean, and given to conservative frowns.

They both were given to loving me.

An Issue
of Mind

Holidays of all sorts are occasions when foodstuffs for varied tastes
are prepared. Eating is a sheer delight. Candies and cookies provide
delectable snacks, as do delightfully arranged nuts—Hickory nuts,
Macadamia nuts, Pistachio nuts, Brazil nuts, Pine nuts, Cashew nuts,
and Almost nuts. The last variety can lead to Cracked nuts which
abound, not in discreetly placed small dishes, but... somewhere.

A Nut in the Woods

I do wonder. I do wonder why? I do wonder why mental health facilities, especially those in large medical centers, are given quite distinctive names, when compared to other parts of the hospital? I've seen signs for pediatric, obstetric, cardiac, intensive care, and emergency wards. These are all good descriptive names. They are all "OK" names. However, one other ward is decidedly different. The appearance of a dull-gray, locked, metal door to that particular area is a definite visual indicator that all is "not OK" behind that entrance. Such wards are often called "halls." The term, hall, is also an indicator that all is "not OK." I have (yes, really) heard of Spruce Hall, Oak Hall, Maple Hall, and Aspen Hall. Note: There is not a Quaking Aspen Hall. That just would be too descriptively offensive. Tree names seem very popular for mental health wards. I know. I had contact with one such facility—a gathering of dendrites called Wood Hall. Extreme stress from my work, panic about my stability, and fear of my thoughts caused me to voluntarily seek help there. However, I felt, shall we say, unduly incarcerated in Wood Hall. There were no lush, juicy peaches or apricots in that place. No,... just the nuts resided in Wood Hall.

I also wonder why many members of the mental health staff in these tree-halls often patronize their charges. "Come now and get down off your tree, er... bed." "Yes, that's very good. You selected the right dining tray." "Be sure to eat all your delicious food, hon." "Oh, be a nice soul, dear, and turn off your light. It's sleepy-time." I am told exactly what to do and when to do it. The staff members don't seem to grasp that not all things can be done on their arbitrarily designated schedules. "Excuse me, it takes me more than 5-minutes to take my shower!" Of course, some order is necessary for taking medication—rhymes with dedication—at 7:00, 11:00, 5:00, 9:00. But, I do wonder about the need for a shuffiing cattle-call to the iron-barred enclosed nurses' station to receive the pills, for ills. "Now remember, be a good patient and get in line alphabetically." Remember... Remember? Is the last name first? Is the first name last? What is my name? Oh, yeah, I'm the one on the forget-me-not drug. And, what I receive is not to be called a "drug"—for which I may be hugged or mugged. It is a "medication." Also, I notice that the pills—the medications—are so anti-everything. I'm here for a positive, pro-experience to improve my mental health. So, what are these anti-anxiety, anti-depression, anti-psychotic, anti's all about? It all sounds so negative. I wonder if there is a pill for the anti-Christ?... Hm-m...

Most tree-halls offer ("offer" means I better darn well participate) their inhabitants a form of occupational therapy. Accompanied by key-chain-rattling staff members, I and my fellow inmates exit our tree-hall abode and parade down a "regular" corridor to a special instruction room. I am sans shoes, just in stocking feet, so I do not wander away. I hold up my beltless jeans with one hand. I grasp my blue-and-white striped baggy robe with the other hand. I am dressed-up for my mental health days. To the casual hospital visitor, it's obvious I am not quite right. I lean a little to the left. Oh, it's not a political thing. It's those drugs, er... medications.

Just what occupation is planned for me provides some concern. It is February. So, I am taught how to cut out— with a child's dull, rounded-point, scissors—slightly skewed, red hearts. If I wish to please those who carefully watch over me, I may Crazy-Glue lacy, white, paper doilies onto the hearts. The male patients, in their stupor, find this activity to be a particularly fruitful, or nut-ful, occupation.

At some point during our time "out," a smiling, cheery staffer, wearing a glowing, immaculately white uniform hands a faded, pink smock to each of us. "Now, put them on, everyone." I really do wonder what is coming now. Ah-ha... it is art time with blunt crayons, a few icky-colored pale pastel sticks, and fine quality newsprint. "We are going to create art!" She states this with far too much enthusiasm. Rembrandt, Monet, and Van Gogh would be pleased—well, maybe not Van Gogh. There was that absent ear, his mind-set, and all. Picasso, on the other hand, might enjoy the captives' artistic interpretations. I use the pastels and execute— ah, must watch that word—create a clumsy scene of green tree, blue lake, green bush, and blue-green sky. "Oh, how imaginative and stunning your artwork is. We'll post it on the wall for all to see what they can do!" All I see are frowns and snarly expressions from my imprisoned cohorts who think I'm a freakin' brown-noser. I really do need an anti-something-or-other now. Review of my "out there" occupation as a professor has no place in this tree-hall. In my estimation, this occupational therapy is just another name for keep-'em-busy garbage. I do not plan to make odd-shaped, red-and-white, doily hearts, even in a second life. And,

"Michael's" and "Hobby-Lobby" are not hiring those of my skill level right now. There is just no interest.

Speaking of lack of interest… I find that we who are in this hoosegow tree-hall quickly lose contact with the non- nut world. "Seinfeld" re-runs, which no one seems to understand, air on the ancient RCA television set. The din of "nothing" pre-empts all newscasts. Earthquakes, wars, melting ice caps—even with New York City now flooded two- feet-higher—have no listeners. The only break in the silent, interminable, and I mean really never-ending, card game is "Gin!"

So, I sit in an old, brown, leather chair in my institutional-green room, again dressed in my baggy robe, waiting and waiting, for—I have no idea. I may have forgotten once more. "Are you feeling OK?" I mutter something unintelligible about not being sure. "Not sure?" queries the staff-techy in an accusatory manner. "Well, you just go put together a puzzle. You'll feel lots and lots better, won't you?" She urges me to extricate myself from my chair. Then, this sheriff secures my elbow, so I don't deviate from her plan, as I reluctantly amble to the activity-dining area. I select a puzzle from several offerings. Like all of them, the pieces are old and worn. I pause. I think I would feel better if the techy and I could sit down to discuss my problems, or even have a simple chat about the weather or Presidents' Day. She sees my hesitancy to jump into my puzzling work. "You really shouldn't be uncooperative." That assessment means adding or taking away drugs, er… medications. So, I really get busy on that scene of a barn roof and half a cow. I have no idea of the complete picture. The box lid is missing.

I do wonder now about being in this hallowed-hall. Perhaps, in some crazed—poor word choice again— moment, I thought this place would help me. Doubts are looming. I do know I want my life to be different. Is it a fantasy to assume that my doctor will sit down with me in comfortable wing-back chairs to discuss my future as we sip a bit of Earl Grey? Well, I have learned all about that word "assume." I get to see the doctor only through wire- mesh glass windows of the nurses' compound. I smile and wave and knock to get attention. I get it from the glowering staff members who form a protective phalanx around the chart-reading head of this tree-hall.

Oh,... I do wonder, once again. The staff has now decided that I am to be assisted to become more "positive." My status as a 45-year-old nut merits me young, and I mean really young, persons quite inexperienced with life. My social workers—a pink-cheeked fellow, and a pink-blushed maiden—come to me with forced smiles. "How are we today?" I think for a moment. We? Oh, you mean me and my other six, Sybil-like, personalities? But such an astute thought is put aside. I answer, "I am fine." Hm-m... It's tricky to articulate "fine," because I'm gronked out on Elysian contentment pills. I want to ask why the social workers' eyes keep crossing. This is funny. I begin to giggle; but, funny is not acceptable. So, I just smile—a little crooked-like. The medicine from the secretive doctor is getting to me. But, what the heck,... it makes me an interesting subject. During subsequent encounters, this team finally begins to approach my life options. I try to articulate, "I have a Ph.D. I am a professor." more often. But, they keep focusing on vocational courses I can take at a local community college. Their excited chatter about creating a career for me brings on depression and a sense of aloneness.

Oh, incredible joy, hooray, hooray, they have a surprise for me today! Three people enter the interrogation, er... conference room at the behest of the social workers. Grief, to see outsiders, to permit them to enter the nut-hall, makes me really wonder. Am I becoming better—whatever that means? Am I becoming positive—whatever that means? "You look very good." God, I hope so. I think I combed my graying hair and put on clean, white socks this morning. One of the trio—the one smiling warmly—asks, "Are you doing well?" I pause. I speak ever-so-clearly, and say, "I am well." The outlanders, who are my friends, and the unseasoned social-work-duo don't realize that I have been in a well. And, if I don't get out soon… out of this well of a nut–hall… well. But, I smile. I chuckle at the right moments as they speak. One well-intentioned friend asks, "Will you be well, if you leave here?" The subtext of the question is: Will you hurt yourself? I think for a moment. Yes, I will be hurting myself if I stub my big toe. But I am sure that's not what is meant, so I remain silent about that toe-thought. The question is asked again. I affirmatively nod my head. Yes.

Because of my response, and because I more frequently and positively sprinkle "return to my profession" into conversations, I am allowed, finally, to depart—to climb down from the tree-hall. I do not mind this exit. I did mind—being watched over as a weak and flawed mental case. I did mind— being unsure of my actions. For a time, I did mind—being. However, that last thought comes only at rare moments. Moments further and further apart. The panic has abated. The fear has eased. I smile as I banish arcane attitudes, tedious television, hangdog hearts, and purposeless puzzles. I am definitely out of the woods. I am now far away from any tree-halls. There are no more nuts.

But, sometimes I still do wonder.

Negative events in the past and in the present may bring a multitude of anxious feelings. And, that anxiety may easily cause fear. That fear can quickly allow our thoughts to spiral down into our dark black hole. Contrary to what is often said, the darkness may be protective and restore what otherwise cannot be repaired. From the darkness, we become able to see.

Searching for Sanity

The sharp-edged panic remained hour after hour. There were brief moments of calm with normal breathing, and logical thought. Then, in seconds, the glazed stare, the rapid breathing, and the anxiety-driven thoughts rushed back in, flooding every feeling with fear. During an afternoon appointment, a psychologist discerned that the panic and the serious desire to escape it were almost beyond control. Calls were made. Notification to the official personnel at the university provided medical leave. Request for private hospitalization was made and granted. Selection of a person to provide security and to drive to the hospital was arranged.

I was the person for whom all was being done "to notify, to request, to select." I was the person filled with extreme suicidal ideation, close to the act itself. I was the person desperately in need of assistance to prevent that act. And so, on a late August afternoon, Katherine persuaded me to pack clothes and to ride with her to a rather pleasant suburb of Columbus, Ohio. Katherine, a fellow professor at the university was one among a close group of concerned friends who had felt helpless as they watched me spiral into my hell.

As Kate began the drive and headed southeast from the village, my mental health was anything but healthy. The panic and fear of what I was doing rose and subsided in ocean-like forms: Panic that my career might end, even with a strong record as a tenured professor. Panic that my past did not matter to those who held out-of-date concepts of mental illness as immoral or weak-minded. Panic that an old colleague believed my mental health record merited my replacement, despite accomplishments. In moments of calm rationality during the trip toward Columbus, Kate and I chatted positively about my seeking a "new self," one assured and confident, one not afraid that I couldn't be "good enough" for any endeavor, even having friends.

The sun set. Kate drove on in descending darkness. That departure of light I equated with my life's demise. The closer we came to our destination, the more I knew my black hole was swallowing me forever. As we covered the last part of the trip to the hospital, Kate got lost for a time. Ironically, I found the predicament extremely funny. Here I was seeking help, but I couldn't get close to it. That bit of humor turned quickly to panic, fear, and my death-wish when Kate found the hospital grounds. Finally, at 9:00 p.m., Kate and I were admitted through the gate to the mental hospital, attributed to be an excellent psychiatric facility. Again, I felt a certain humorous irony. Here I was wanting to die, yet I was accepting entrance to a place bent on preventing my death.

A kind, uniformed guard escorted Kate and me into a pleasantly-appointed facility with comfortable, chocolate- brown leather chairs and sofas. Pastel-colored pillows, which I assumed were carefully placed, further softened the atmosphere. An aide brought slices of cheese, crackers, and hot herbal tea as we waited for the "intake interview." Panic grew though.

I wanted Kate's assurance and promise that she would not abandon me, if I refused to stay at this place. Then, someone I sensed as warm-hearted, kind, and caring came in to interview me. I truly felt OK, until she introduced herself as the emergency admitting psychologist. Panic again, when I heard the word "emergency." This was not a casual let's-just-get-to-meet-you conversation. What is your full name? Can you tell me your date of birth? Who is the President? What is the current day and year? Do you think you could hurt yourself? The questions went on and on. Thoughts began to blur as the fear and panic took over, completely. The void I felt lasted forever, it seemed. Calming voices from Kate and the doctor sought to bring me back to the reality of reading, accepting, and signing the forms for voluntarily admitting myself to this hospital.

Once the "signing tasks" were completed, the uniformed gentleman asked Kate and me to follow him to my residence-to-be. She did so, and we came to one of several buildings called "cottages." It was now 11:30 p.m. I had accepted, with reservation, my admission to a mental hospital. Kate was required to leave me at the entrance. I could say nothing, but gave Kate a "Please don't leave me." look. She gave me a brief hug and departed with, "You'll be OK. Just hang in there. We'll all be in touch shortly." Actually, neither they nor I would be able to "be in touch" for fourteen days. That implacable rule was part of the admission and treatment plan.

When I entered the foyer, I met the night-shift psychiatric nurse Sue, a thin, forty-ish, assured professional attired in brown slacks and a soft, yellow sweater—definitely not a stiff, starched, white uniform. A young psych-tech. also met me, and asked to take my luggage to what would be "my" room. Sue wanted to ask more questions about why I had come; but, by that time, 12:30 a.m., my fears and exhaustion muddled all my thoughts. She and the tech gently took me to get ready for bed. Then, Sue sat beside me talking softly as though I were a child needing comfort to doze off. I did begin something akin to fitful sleep. Every fifteen minutes, I awoke cowering in fear when someone opened the door and shined a light on me to check my condition. I was on suicide watch.

That agonizing night ended at 7:00 a.m., when the almost effusive day-nurse came to welcome me to "Aspen Cottage." Ginnie suggested that I put on my robe and come have a bite of breakfast in the meeting-dining area. Only two of us were served from the steam-cart. I quickly realized I was seen as an unsafe patient when I was given only plastic utensils and a paper plate and cup. I learned that the other cottage residents had gone outside for breakfast in the cafeteria, and for exercise in the gym. No such privileges belonged to me. And, I felt as if I had been introduced to the front of an 18-wheeler Mack truck. Food of any sort had no appeal that morning. Yet, my old "need to please" surfaced, and I smilingly nibbled on a sweet-roll, which I washed down with acidic, black decaffeinated coffee. While I ate, two psych-techs nonchalantly asked me more and more questions to learn "everything" about me. They knew the answers; they simply wanted to test my alertness and awareness of my surroundings and actions. With a modicum of clarity, I responded; then, took them aback when I began to "interrogate" them about their own work.

The techs shared much about the structure of what was called the hospital "campus," and its facilities. The cottages looked like large chalk-white, wood-sided homes with gray-black shingle roofs. Each cottage—with a tree or flower name—had two wings of bedrooms for male and female residents. Youth, under age eighteen, who suffered from anxiety, depression, anorexia, bulimia, or suicidal tendencies resided in Oak Cottage. My cottage held adults with similar mental and physical problems. There were "quiet areas" for reading, writing, thinking. Sitting alone in one's room was discouraged. The cottage also had a TV-viewing room, the meeting-dining room, the usual bathroom facilities, and the office-station from which medications and assorted orders were given. The second floor had a group activity room, a triple bank of public phones, and the secretive, locked, meeting room for the staff. Two small, confining rooms were available for doctor-patient "chats."

The grounds had large grassy areas, now filled with trees and shrubs in beautiful red and gold fall foliage. A store for sundries and cigarettes, a brightly-lit cafeteria and music building, and a fully-equipped gym with a basketball court occupied one-third of the grounds. All were nicely secluded by large maple trees and fire-bushes that belied the size of the features. A medical building with exam, MRI, EEG, and ECT rooms was attached to another striking structure occupied by the well-appointed offices for the assorted M.D.s with their assorted specialties.

All the information muddied my mind; but, I sensed I would become aware far too soon of what had been described. After my limited plastic breakfast, complete with Jeopardy-like queries, the techs helped me unpack and store my luggage for the extended visit. They urged me to shower, make my bed, and strive for a sense of normalcy in a place that was nowhere near normal to me. Panic and fear again viciously grabbed and controlled my behavior that first day. I strongly felt that nothing was going to help my mental state. I just sat in an overstuffed-chair listening to my thoughts, and occasionally responding to questions and directives by the staff. The other "experienced" residents left me alone in my black hole.

The second day at the mental hospital began much like the first. The plastic breakfast with coffee minus caffeine contributed to a dull headache. I was ever so closely observed. Anything, any object that had potential for self-harm, was taken from my belongings. Even a simple cardboard wildlife bookmark was removed. That action left me with a certain violated feeling. A piece of limp paper became its substitute. The major activity for me that day involved a complete blood work-up and a physical exam. I was led, "accompanied" so the staff said, to the medical building by a tech. She made the uneasy walk more like a stroll through the woods. Sandy helped me keep control of the waves of panic and fear as we drew closer to my tests. After the lengthy, extremely thorough check-up, which brought spasms of uncontrollable panic, Sandy again aided me with a return walk to the cottage, careful to keep me from lurching toward the entrance gate. Viewing "Star Trek: The Next Generation" offered change from the frightening exam, and hope that there would not be another plastic dinner. Then, numbness set in for the rest of the day and evening. "Lights Out" for bedtime offered no respite. There had been no talk with the staff about my condition. I still jerked violently awake in fear when checked throughout the night.

Mid-morning of day three finally brought a visit by an appointed psychiatrist, who seemed in a hurry to review my background, and read the assessment notes by all the nurses, techs, and staff. This doctor informed me that he was immediately taking away my current medications. He further told me, in an almost accusatory tone, I would be unable to have them while at the hospital. In my state of anxiety, I inferred he thought I was some kind of addict. However, at that same session, he said that I was to decide if I wanted to try Prozac for my mental problems. I was aware the medication was new, and there were concerns regarding its efficacy and potential dangers. Of course, my "desire to please" prompted me to tell this impeccably-dressed, Mercedes-driving, intimidating doctor to prescribe what he thought was best. But, I was upset, incredibly furious inside myself, that this pompous "helper" had the audacity to place such a decision on my plate at this time. Perhaps, my fury was connected to the confusion and fear regarding any new medication. The entire issue negatively impacted our therapeutic relationship for the few subsequent times we met.

Each day of that first week involved close supervision by the staff. On the one hand, I appreciated the kindness and care when I was trying to be a "good enough" patient for them. On the other hand, I seethed that I was being watched openly and surreptitiously, that plastic dinnerware was part of my dining pleasure, and that I couldn't be left alone in my room. I wanted these actions to cease. Although I knew they were in place to help me, I still desperately wanted my life to cease.

Certain privileges were granted during each of the following weeks of my time at the hospital. A few "coulds" were allowed. If a tech. was with me, I could sit on the front porch of the cottage with the other residents. I could attend group therapy sessions which focused on our future "outside life" skills, such as getting a job, and learning to work with other people. I felt strongly that such topics meant a total loss of my valuable thinking time, self-absorbed though it was. But, I played a game, and added comments that made me appear as if I were getting better. I could walk in line with the residents to the cafeteria for an abundance of over-cooked vegetarian meals. I could attend a music class where I was to re-learn how to play the dulcimer. An over-zealous staff member had discovered that I once was proficient on the instrument. However, my frustrated mind did not allow the necessary coordination to play it again. In addition, tremors in my hands, about which no one seemed concerned, developed. The uncontrollable shaking even hampered my ability to eat— to hold forks and spoons, cups and plates. I begged out of the lessons, the cost for which was to come from my own pocket. My desire did not please the instructional staff who thought that I was just avoiding becoming well.

The last "could" permitted me to have only two guests during one week in the latter part of my stay. A wonderful couple, now retired from our university, came from Columbus to visit me. Dan had made his mark as both excellent professor and administrator. Beth, his kind, caring, and giving wife, and I had worked together with many young women in a highly regarded national honor society. These two people were ideal role models for the university students. For a little more than an hour, I struggled to sound and appear well and stable as I listened to them. They chatted about my past work at the school, and all the potential future work in teaching communication courses and creating readers theatre productions. I had loved working with that couple, both in educational and social capacities. But, at that moment, I believed I was failing them by being hospitalized. I fought tears in order to smile and say I was improving by leaps-and-bounds. Even my words seemed trite, flat, and stupid as my self-loathing increased.

The self-anger, self-hatred, and self-destructive parts of my being never fully left. I kept them carefully hidden. In a way, I did feel safe, safe at least from the violent thoughts that might surface in action. The numerous hours the staff spent in group sessions with the residents discussing self-esteem and how to be "happy with ourselves" didn't prove advantageous to my image as a professor at that time. However, the staff observed my outward actions and reactions as positive progress. I was pleased that they were pleased. I tried to "be well," to do and say the "right things;" but, inside I still felt the seduction of the black vortex. Of this, they knew nothing.

The staff also appeared especially unaware of the turmoil caused by phone calls with my parents who still resided in Colorado. At this time, I so much wanted them to provide emotional support. My attempts to seek understanding met with denigrating criticism of my career, my friends, my life. To them, I was weak, basically a failure in all I had done. Perhaps, they had no other way to express their concerns. Unfortunately, their words confirmed aloud what I held in silence.

The dichotomy of external appearance and inner turmoil was part of my daily fight. The few minutes spent once a week with the psychiatrist were unrewarding and tedious. I felt "categorized" and "dismissed" with: "She's depressed, give her Prozac, and she'll be fine." I did not know what would happen once I was on the medication which he now prescribed. I knew it took time for psychotropic medications to begin to work. I also knew I had little time to see if it did work for me. Thirty days was all that my insurance plan allowed for mental health hospitalization. The four weeks were soon to end and I would have to re-enter the outside world in some sane form. I tried focusing on the assistance of the staff, believing that if I tried hard enough the inner-sensations of negativity would dissipate. However, I just felt inside that I was not taught how to handle the disruptive feelings. So, I continued to function—to eat, to talk, to sleep—in as normal a fashion as I could. But, there was always that "but," I still felt that my demons—my "Furies"—were there at the edge of a projected calm demeanor.

Day 30. The day of discharge arrived. Gloomy, windy, and icy cold snow flurries reflected my mood. I felt numb as I prepared to leave. As much as I had disliked being there, the hospital had offered a modicum of safety. My thoughts had roamed in dangerous places; but, I had not acted on them. That was the only accomplishment I could accept. So, on that Saturday, Kate returned to drive me home. To embrace my friend, to be in a car, to see forests and fields brought feelings that calmed the negativity for a time. Once beyond the institution's gates, I immediately asked Kate to stop at some restaurant for a double-double cheeseburger, fries, and a super-sized black coffee. Kate paused and looked at me with a strange expression. I hurriedly explained that I now had gained my freedom—from decaf coffee, and the hospital's monotonous, incredibly bland, genuinely dreadful, vegetarian burgers. We found a nearby Wendy's. I ate. I smiled. I laughed as Kate related stories of people and events at school and in the village. For a brief moment, I relished the experience. Finally, with mugs of coffee in hand, we left the restaurant and headed back toward home. We were returning at the same time of day as when we left a month before. Kate did not get lost this time.

As Kate drove, silence began to descend, just as the darkness did. Kate glanced over at me to ask if I was OK. "No." I said to her concerned question. "I'm not sure what OK means anymore, Kate. I'll try to be as stable as I can. I know I want to teach again, to direct again, to return for Winter Quarter." Nothing was said for some miles. Then, I tried, I dared to tell her. "Kate, the inner fury that made me move toward the black hole is still with me. Four weeks at that place has not altered or banished that deep, dark inside. Perhaps, no amount of time there ever would have." I asked Kate to try to understand, to accept, that at times

I might come near the vortex. "But, at the hospital, didn't you… didn't they…" I stopped her question. "No, Kate…" I paused for a moment. "I'm still trying to find some kind of sane vision for my life…. I think I'll be searching for a long time."

*Password, Boggle, Scattergories, Zig-Zag, Scrabble. All of these
names, and many others, are titles for word games which have long
held a fascination for adults and children. Dedicated lovers of the
games find them, not only fun, but also mind-enriching and even
therapeutic. Such is true in the following glimpse of one game.*

The Word Game

Hello, little one. May we sit together? I think today is a good day for us
to chat with each other. No, no… do not be afraid. Come sit with me in
the cave of grass you have built—to protect you. The tall, emerald-green
grass waves so gently around us. Here… take a sprig of this—our—grass.
Now, put the end in your mouth, chew on it a bit, then suck out the sweet-
flavored juice. It's fun, isn't it? Here, take another one. Ah, we might just
sit here and pluck and chew on our grass all day.

You ask what, little one? What day is this that we sit here? Why, it's
Tuesday. Oh, no—wait, wait… hold on to me. Let me hold on to you.
Sh-sh, now. You're remembering that vicious time, those horrible days—
those Tuesdays. Here… sit in my lap. Let me tell you a story about Tuesday.
Just listen now.… You see, the word Tuesday comes from an old, terribly
ancient name for a god of war. His name was "Tew" which sounds like
"phew—a really stinky funny sound. See, little one, "Tew" is just a word,
and the word cannot hurt you. When you think of Tuesday, just think
quickly of funny, old, smelly Tew running around being all angry with the
world!… It is a word to laugh at, isn't it?

Now, listen again for a moment. The day after Tuesday is Wednesday... right? Well, Wednesday is a name for "Wodin's" day. Wodin was the head-honcho god who told Tew when to "chill-out" and calm down. Guess now about Thursday. The next day? Yes, that's right. Well, that word is for "Thor." He went around making it rain, banging his big hammer—boom—boom— making loud thunder. Although it can sound scary, it's just a word, too.... Ah, little one, now we come to our special day—Friday. Why is it so special? Listen closely. Friday is named for "Fria." She is the goddess of love—love for all things: kitties, puppies, wooly lambs, and trees, flowers, our very own green grasses. And, best of all, love for you—my love for you always. So, when you think of the word Friday, think and remember our special day of love.

I really like the word "Fria." Oh, you do, too? Let's just sit here for a bit more, and chew on some grass. Why don't we also chew on some other words and thoughts you have—and words and thoughts I have. Sometimes we are afraid of word-thoughts we don't really understand. What do I mean? Well... let's play a game. Yes, little one... a game. You tell me a word, a thought. Then, I'll tell you one.

OK, here goes our game. You first.... "Hurt," you say? Ah, that's a big hard word for such a little girl. Tell me more.... You say you "hurt" from your head to your toes? You say people caused you to "hurt." Let me tell you, little one, that "hurt" you feel, that you agonizingly remember was wrong—a great big wrong. Here... come closer. Let me tell you, no one should ever have such hurt—ever. Those who hurt you were "evil." Do you know what I mean by evil? It's a really black nasty word. You do know, you say? Ah, you understand so much—far too much.

Here, have a sprig of grass, and tell me more words. What? Ah-ha…
you want *my* word-thought. You're clever. I hoped I could get you to tell all
your words. OK… I'll play fair. "Good"—that's my word. Yes… good like
popsicles and ice cream and, yes, sprinkles on the ice cream. But, "good"
also means to be kind, to care. You are right. Those who hurt you were not
good, even though they said they were. Little one, I have known good—
the good shown by our beautiful mother Elaine, and by Grandmother and
Grandfather. You remember, don't you? Yes, they were truly good. And
like you, I have known those people who only thought and said they were
good. We have had a difficult time in our lives with the word good, haven't
we? Sometimes figuring out meanings of words confuses us. But, you
know, little one, that you are good! You always have been and always will
be. Always, you ask? Yes, always. We shall be "good" together. You and I.

Now, it's your turn to share a word-thought. H-m-m… Why do you
clench your small fists so tight, and frown so hard? Is "Anger" your word?
I think you don't want to say the word; but, you are telling me the word
with your "body-talk." Tell me, though, what you are thinking right now.
You seem angry, really angry deep inside. Tell me about that anger. Oh…
it's about that man and woman? I think, my child, I can understand that
deep anger. And, you say, you are angry because no one came to help you.
Not your Daddy. Not your Grandfather. Not even your Grandmother.
In some way, yes, they should have known. But, what happened—your
horrible, sad secret—was hidden from them. And… go on. You are angry
at me for not helping you escape the fear and pain? Oh, my little one, I was
not there, because I was not yet. I was not as I am now. I do know what
happened to you, and I have begun to tell your terrible, ghastly story, so
you may come to know love and security. I could beg you not to be angry;

but, you have every right to your feelings—and anger can be one of those feelings.... Go ahead, now. Allow the feeling—the anger—to be. Don't hide it anymore... not anymore. Do not bury your anger or cover it with a black-ish old blanket. No, instead, think of a beautiful cloak with an emerald-green lining—like your grasses— allowing you to be free, to know you are loved. No more black. Let it go away, little one. It is not a color for you, nor is it mine for you. You see... I, too, have known anger. I hate that man and woman. I also know anger at other unprotective, untruthful, and unloving people. For now though, this is your place and your time. Little one, I am glad you can share this feeling, the word-thought of anger with me. It is good that you do. Please, oh please, never forget that I can listen and care.

My small friend, I sense there is another word-thought you wish to say. I will give up my turn so you can share it. Come... say your word-thought. It is bad, you say? No... we, you and I, can talk about it amidst our tall, safe grasses. Come now... what is the word? You are telling me it is "Shame?" Oh, little one, you should not even know that word. But, you say *you* feel shame? Why, my child? Because of what those people—the two evil ones—did to you? You feel shame because they hurt you and you did nothing? Oh, dear little one, you had no choice. You could do nothing against their evil. There is no need to think even for a tiny minute that you should feel shame. They— the evil ones—are to be "shamed"... shamed for all that they were. They were so shameful in their actions that there is no word, not one, of good to say about them. So... please, please, do not feel shame.

May I tell you I think I understand your strong feelings about shame? You see, my favorite little person, I—yes, I—have felt shame because I was not there to save you from the evil ones. Also, as I grew, I was made to feel shame for being "adopted," shame for not being "good enough," shame sometimes for just "being." So, you see, I do not ever want you to feel shame. I think, as we sit here in your beautiful grasses, that together you and I might make a special agreement—a pact, we'll call it. You and I must think very carefully about that word "shame." Are you following what I say? Good.… Now, let's sit here and "see" ourselves not ever feeling shame, not ever using that word-thought about ourselves. Close your eyes as I close mine. And, we'll see ourselves with no shame.

Shall we hold hands, little one? Let's hold tightly to one another and never let go. Yes… you and I, we, are safe. Yes, today our "word-thought" game has been difficult for you—for both of us. Yet, we must both remember that we can smile together. We can laugh together. We can love together. And, my dear little one, remember always with happiness that you are deep inside me—and—I am with you. That is our present… and our future.

Sometimes no words can be found to introduce ideas, feelings,
or thoughts. These must simply stand on their own.

My Child... My Little One

I know, my child. I know of your cave of grass. I know you wove tall, soft, emerald-green strands to form this place—a place of solace. You created a space, a haven from those who called themselves "caregivers."

You suffered much, my little one, at the hands of the man who called you "Sweetie," at the hands of the woman who called you "Honey." You knew there was no genuine love in their words of supposed affection. "Hey, Sweetie, come inside the house so we can play." "Now, Honey, don't dawdle. We have a wonderful surprise for you." There was never any surprise. But, you had to obey. You had to go to them. You had to. You knew by rote what occurred on the same day of every week, of every month. And so, when they took you, you shut your eyes as tightly as you could. Yet, you saw—you saw, heard, felt. As the minutes crept by, your mind, your thoughts, and your feelings shut down. You uttered no cry. You simply endured the vicious, horrific behavior of those two people.

Then came more fear. Again and again there was the ritual. "Aw, Honey, you did good." she would murmur repulsively. "Sweetie, you're something special." he would utter menacingly. Last came the sickening threat of the "little chat." Together they spoke, "Don't you ever, ever dare tell anyone about our play time. It's our special secret. Remember, if you do, you will die." With that warning said, you turned to leave the house.

"Oh, Honey… Sweetie, don't forget, we love you." Their calculated smiles followed you to the door.

You did not run from them. You walked slowly and deliberately to the nearby old apple orchard to sit on the frayed rope swing. You waited for a time to be certain they no longer watched you. Only then did you slip away through the trees to your cave of grass. You knelt, sat, curled onto your side in pain and fear. In some way, you listened in peace to the cool rustling breezes that finally would bring you the refuge of sleep. It is in this cave of comfort I have found you.

Please, do not run from me in fear. I come not to hurt you. I come in grief for you. I come to take away your torment. I come to kneel with you, to sit by you, to curl-up beside you in your cave of grass. You see, my child, I want to show you, to give to you another place of safety and security, a different place of your favorite emerald-green which will protect you from suffering and sadness. I want to share the place of shelter and goodness with you, my little one.

You will find no pain, no fear, no grief in that place. There you will find rest in the grasses which also wave in the fresh breezes. You may run in those soft grasses, roll over and over in them, gently caress the long thin stems, and stroke them through the fingers of your little hands. You may turn to look up to the vast sky, and in amazement see the curving, arching colors of red, orange, yellow, green, blue, indigo, violet—a rainbow of joy for you.

There, also, you will find a rainbow of deep affection from seven wonderful companions. Their presence will be watchful concern, care, and safekeeping in which you may fully trust. These splendid companions have come here to this place of grasses, to this place of comfort, to always support you, and to believe in you. Some you will, in time, know as your wonderful grandmother, as your joyful little burro, as your guiding teacher, as your courageous great spirit bear, as your incomparable mentor.

And, especially in this place, you will find love through and in one being who stands slightly apart from the circle of companions. You will be drawn toward her stunning radiance, yet hesitate to approach. However, amidst that brilliance, she will gently motion for you to come close. As you do so, you will see her attired in a cloak of royal-blue velvet, bordered by ribbons of golden thread. You will pause. She will smile, and urge you to come nearer. She slowly will open, and unfold the cloak to reveal a lining of satin— emerald-green glistening satin—the emerald-green of your beloved grasses that formed your secret cave of solace. You will know this stately being is true, unconditional love. She will smile warmly, tenderly. And, she will wrap the cloak around you in the most extraordinary expression of love you have ever known. And, you will be embraced and know peace and believe in love.

You may turn to me, I who have brought you from your cave of grasses. You may pause and with your questioning eyes ask, "Why... why do you do this?" And, I shall say, "Because, my child, you are me—and—I am you."

Whether we go gently or fight a thrashing battle, we must eventually leave, or pass from, this estate we have inhabited. What happens beyond that moment, we cannot see. What happens before, we can see—and it may be terribly distressing or terribly delightful.

Funerals and the Wicked Witch

I want to write about death for a moment. To be more specific, I want to write about funerals. According to my calculations, no one likes funerals. Funeral directors, however, have been known to appreciate them. Sad, morose, depressing—such adjectives describe many funerals. Not many folk depart a funeral stepping lively to "The Colonel Bogey March," or even better, humming "Everything's Coming Up Roses." "What a swell funeral!" is seldom overheard.

Now, I understand that memorial services can be less deadly. Perhaps, that last word isn't altogether appropriate; because, someone once known to the attendees is, indeed, dead. Kind, warm, and loving remarks may envelop all; words of praise, honor, and tribute may extol the life of the dead one. During some memorial services, rambling remarks may convey huzzahs and hurrahs for the absent soul. Open laughter can occur, as can respectful chuckles. Of course, the chuckles might turn into weeping and wailing. Simply recall Mary Tyler Moore's breakdown in the television episode honoring "Chuckles the Clown."

Celebrations of the lives of the dead are sometimes a bit oxymoron-oriented. Can there be a sad cheer, a dim glow, a quiet acclamation? Yet, a growing number of folk are requesting that everyone attending "have a good time," that they affirmatively express joy of a life, and that they refer to the death as a passing to another state of being. There is to be no reference to dead, gone, or kaput. There still can be, in some quarters (think, French), a band playing and people singing (think, "When the Saints Come Marching In"). In some locales, telling wild stories and jokes—related or unrelated to the one who has passed—are accompanied by free-flowing alcoholic beverages. And, everybody has a damned fine time, so much so that the following day may bring no recollection that an associate did pass.

The primary thought to keep in mind is that all three forms of remembrance may provide an ease of pain, a hint of joy, and a sense of closure. Speaking personally, I don't like thinking about my first funeral encounter with a lot of sad people in a big old church. On that occasion, I was swatted on my bottom, and thunked on my head. I think I was squirming and whispering—a lot. I just wanted to go home to find my mommy who had disappeared a few days before. During the second experience, my behavior was far more subdued. I was nine-years-old, and the person mourned was my devoted, steadfast, Grandmother Roberts, suddenly gone after an horrific car accident. I felt a distinct loss. I did not know from where or from whom stability would come in my young life. I did not cry.

When the high school typing teacher died, a service was held in the auditorium, which was also the school basketball court. Relatives, townspeople, and teachers attended. Of course, we high school students were invited, urged, required to go in a show of support. Now, I know that a significant number of the young men would rather have wrapped their fingers around a basketball, than have held their fingers poised for touch-typing for the young teacher. As much as the students admired her, the event provided a jim-dandy break from afternoon classes. Touching? Yeah.

After that occasion, I began missing funerals, which were really drawn-out, depressive, affairs. No celebration joy in them. Grandfather Roberts, Grammy Black, Aunt Vi, Uncle Ray, and other assorted relatives and friends of the family who passed away lived in Colorado. I lived in Ohio. I did not attend the funerals because I could not leave the classes I taught at the university at those particular times. I simply could not. Yet, a whole lot of anger was directed toward me for my miscreant ways.

Permit me, for a little bit, to comment on the memorial service for my father. In August, 1995, I flew to Arizona to be with him at St. Luke's hospital. Dad was in the ICU. He knew he was dying, and the excruciating long hours dragged on. Finally, the once vibrant man did find relief from bags, and tubes, and assorted machines. With his death, arranging transport to Colorado fell to my two brothers and me, mostly me. I had the credit card with the highest dollar limit. I felt overwhelmed that the processes of obtaining the minister, selecting a "reasonably-priced" coffin, and writing obituaries for the area papers became my responsibility. I can almost laugh, now, about the silly squabbles over which thank-you notes to choose for the anticipated flowers and gifts. Family members, stressed and saddened, sometimes lost a sense of propriety. My offer for the memorial service was to speak a few heartfelt words about my father's life. At that time, I had taught many forms of public speaking for twenty-five years; however, my gift was refused by my stepmother, complete with a devastating, disparaging diatribe about my lack of knowledge and skills. The memorial service was adequate. Few of his friends attended. Most had already passed away. I was relieved.

Then came death and another service. My stepmother died in February, 2003. She was buried a few days later. I was in Ohio. I did not leave Ohio. A surgery and inability to travel prevented that. Thus, I could not attend the memorial service. I never buried her—physically or emotionally. However, that woman remained in my mind as a formidable instrument hindering my positive functioning. Even when I retired from my teaching career in Ohio and moved to Colorado, the old traumatic cycles of her love, her animosity, and non-acknowledgment behaviors toward me kept crawling to the surface of my mind. Some dear friends kept reminding me that she was dead. She could not hurt me anymore. They also made observations about my having difficulties because I never really buried her.

Such serious thoughts led to an oddly warped sort of humor. From my past came the memory of the people of "Oz" rejoicing that the Wicked Witch was dead. Ding-Dong. My nemesis was dead, too. A "funeral and burial" were suggested by my friends. Cec, an old boarding school roommate, was selected to assist with the special "ceremony." Her warmth, her care, her sincerity guided the preparations. Near my condo, I found a seven-inch- sized, smooth gray rock. I used a black-ink, Sharpie permanent marker to inscribe my stepmother's initials and date of death on it. Cec and I set the "service" time. Then, she called from her home on the western slope of the Rockies. I received the call outside my Denver home. Together, we joined in our funereal work. Cec provided lovely, poetic thoughts. I provided bitter, angry remarks. There we were: Cec on her phone in

Carbondale. I on my phone at the base of the large, full-foliaged, oak tree beneath my second floor living-room window. Still grasping the phone, I knelt and placed the rock between two substantial roots of the tree. At that point, absurdity took over the ceremony. There I was, talking into a phone—in front of a tree. I slowly and clearly described the scene to Cec. The process had a rather Druidic-quality. As I stood, then bent over to secure the "head-stone" with small pebbles, I looked as if I was giving obeisance to a green-leafed deciduous being. A small brown squirrel on a run from a flowering crab tree to an evergreen paused briefly, flicking its tail in wonder, I suppose. Then, a kindly fellow, walking his gray Schnauzer, stopped to ask if all was OK. I solemnly replied that all was just fine. Cec, who heard the exchange, began to chuckle, which gave way to a full-blown fit of laughter. I, also, could no longer maintain any serious demeanor. Still holding her phone, Cec began to chant the famous song from "The Wizard of Oz." Still holding my phone, I followed suit, and echoed the legendary words. The joining of rock, tree, laughter, and song made for wickedly hysterical joy. And, it all provided a moment, a long-needed moment of satisfaction.

"Ding-Dong, the Witch is dead." No…. My conflicted nemesis was dead—and buried. Funeral, memorial service, celebration—all was complete. I had seen an end.

A MATTER
OF FINDING

Do three rows of wooden benches make a church? Do an old, square,
oak table with three worn stools and two tin coffee mugs make a
kitchen? Do a creaky rocking chair and wooden butter churn make
a rustic porch? Do gray-black-colored forms make rocks on a rough
hillside? Yes. They are all as they seem when we audience members
allow our willing suspension of disbelief. We see.... We believe.

Dark of the Theatre

The lights slowly come up on the scene, and focus on down-stage-right. A sad, mournful song begins telling the story about a young "gal" leaving her "muther." A stocky, young fellow in worn, rough-cut, denim overalls, faded red-plaid shirt, and scuffed tan boots, strums the accompanying guitar chords. A tired, over-worked, middle-aged woman plaintively sings the words, her face tilted back in a woeful expression. The feelings come from deep within her soul, as she rocks rhythmically in an old wicker chair, and forces the plunger of the ancient butter churn up and down in time to the music. She wears a washed-out, greenish, floral-print dress made from several old, cotton flour sacks. Her brown shoes are rugged, lace-up, high-tops. Graying strands of hair are held back in a loose bun. Both individuals reflect an image of a time when some hill-folk lived deep in the Appalachian Mountains.

This woman, "Ma," and the boy, "Floyd," are the wife and son of "Pa Allen." Daughter "Barbara," with her flowing, coal-black hair, is the high-spirited, teenage member of the family—always the focus, always the center of attention for the locals. Pa kind of likes her looks. Ma frets over her looks. Floyd is indifferent about her looks. Rolling, misty, wooded hills surround the family's Buck Creek cabin-home. On the nearby promontory of Baldy Mountain resides "John." Local legend calls him "The Witch Boy who flies when the moon is full." John is, indeed, a witch who seeks to become human when he falls in love with Barbara Allen.

Take this complex family situation, and add wild, moonshine-driven dancing by all the neighbors. Further add Bible-thumping, forgiveness-seeking, sin-repenting, and fervent-singing by all the townsfolk. Then, mix all these ingredients into that Appalachian world of jealousy, betrayal, lust, and rape of Barbara Allen by her strong, mean suitor Marvin Hudgens during the revival song, "Washed in the Blood of the Lamb." Once all the mountain-folk have gathered, once all the events have taken place, there emerges the Ballad of Barbara Allen—the groundwork for the play, "Dark of the Moon." The heavy-hearted lyrics, as sung by Ma Allen, continue on in the "churn" scene. Ma fears that this song about the lost girl might turn to reality in the behavior of her daughter. She sees Barbara, who is always flirting enticingly, finding nothing but ill fortune.

The play, "Dark of the Moon," tells only one story of Barbara Allen. There are at least forty-two accounts of the popular fable still told in the backwoods of Appalachia. Adams State College of Colorado staged the Howard Richardson play in the fall of 1967. I had the pleasure of creating the role of Ma Allen that season. For six weeks, the large cast of the play rehearsed hill-dialects, character development, mountain dances by the townsfolk, and group songs by the church congregation.

Ma Allen's sorrowful song "Life's Other Side," the focus of the "churn" scene in the production, turned into an acting challenge for me. Son Floyd plucked the guitar strings harder, and I, as Ma, topped his sounds with even more expressions of dismay related in the rough dialect. The 800-member theatre audience listened raptly, occasionally chuckling softly. Ma Allen continued with the grief and fear and misery, singing of a young girl led into a brothel of sin.

It happened at that point in the song. "It" was a loud, deep, sound from the mid-section of the theatre audience. "Well, isn't this just great. That's my grand-daughter!" In his sonorous voice, my normally highly discreet grandfather had just given his critique of the play, particularly of my performance. He had attended many music and theatre productions during his life, so his outburst was more than unusual. I was aghast. I was mortified. Yet, I wanted to giggle, to laugh with the audience. However, there is a major theatre rule: "Never break character while on stage." It was vital to keep the rhythm of the play moving. So, I closed my eyes, bit the inside of my right cheek, took a breath, and lifted my head high. With more fervor, tainted with forlorn, broken-hearted sadness, Ma Allen concluded that the young thing was never seen again.

The audience applauded energetically, not so much for Ma Allen's musical presentation, I'm sure, but more for my grandfather's unabashed enthusiasm. The lights went down on the scene. Ma Allen exited stage right. In the offstage darkness, I could hardly stifle my own embarrassed laughter, as I collected myself to be ready for my next entrance. I now recall little of what occurred in the scenes that followed. However, my—and Ma Allen's— rendition of that dolorous song has remained with me, indelibly etched in memory. As though it were a lighting instrument, that bright moment of humor provided for me a new vision of a somber and sometimes crusty grandfather.

Critics for the Adams State campus newspaper, and the San Luis Valley Courier wrote only unqualified positive remarks in their articles about "Dark of the Moon"—the creative ensemble, the intriguing characters, and Ma Allen's incomparable vocal interpretation of the mountain song of a lost soul. Such critiques always make an actor feel assured and confidant. Although, in my estimation, "That's my grand-daughter!" topped all that could be written in the papers. In the dark of the theatre that opening night, Grandfather had given his own unmistakable, affirmative review of the play and of Ma Allen.

We saw…. We believed.

Verna Peterson… Norma Peterson. These women were the yin and yang of influence in my early academic career. The roles the two educators played in the strife of my black and white world provided strikingly different visions for success.

Peterson v. Peterson

As I look back and consider a younger time in my life, I see Mrs. Verna Peterson as part of the ancient duality in humankind. This special individual first introduced what became the gratifying, fulfilling, and challenging work of scientific thought and study in my freshman year at our local high school. She began to nurture the interest that had been developing since sixth grade when the seed of my love for the field of medicine began to grow. As an eleven- year-old, my love was for the medical care given by doctors and nurses, when I fought to overcome rheumatic fever during the long summer months leading to the highlight year of elementary school. Similar care provided for the kidney illnesses I had during middle school years further strengthened my desire to have a career in medicine.

By the time I entered Verna Peterson's world of high school biology, stories of medical miracles and breakthroughs had already become embedded knowledge. I consumed books, such as "Microbe Hunters," again and again. Perhaps, the dedicated efforts of Antoni van Leeuwenhoek, Louis Pasteur, and Jonas Salk unconsciously typified my own personal struggles. Histories of women, such as Marie Curie and Elizabeth Blackwell, provided even stronger perspectives on the field of medicine. I just knew I could somehow live a life akin to those of my heroic protagonists.

The tall and stately teacher, who drew respect so easily from her students, closely observed my intense focus on the profession of medicine. I felt a touch of honor when Mrs. Peterson selected me to be one of her lab assistants. She provided out-of-class reading assignments to enhance my skills. She insisted on first-rate research, accompanied with first-rate written work. I know that somewhere stored in an old, cardboard box my study of the deadly disease carried by the African Tsetse Fly must still reside. Peterson's warm smile offered encouragement, and, perhaps, a consistent expression of care that home life did not provide. No doubts about my desire to enter the realms of science, and to become a physician ever clouded our positive student-mentor relationship.

She quite frequently inquired about my work in other courses, for Verna Peterson was a superb teacher who saw the need for students to excel in all subjects. She wanted all of us to become proficient in writing, and coordinated assignments with those who taught English. Challenging our skills in Latin, especially as they applied to scientific terms, was also her forte. Even through times of scalpels thrown into tiled ceilings by the less-than-brilliant class clowns, even through bouts of nausea and vomiting by those students attempting to extricate eyeballs and hearts from formaldehyde-imbued frogs, Mrs. Peterson's subdued, "Oh, really now." brought calm and composure to the class's behavior. With a "Let's not let these things happen, please." she gently ordered the scalpel culprits to detention, and the queasy ones to the nearest restroom. Order prevailed. Dissection continued. Mrs. Peterson did have a finely honed sense of humor, subtle that it was. It seems fair to note the mischievous glint in her eyes during preparations for "lab days."

That deeply significant and rewarding Peterson-world came to an end all too soon. In 1960, family difficulties interrupted my life at that high school. Because of rebellious, unruly, behaviors involving an older family member, I was, oddly enough, the sibling sent to finish my high school education at a boarding school. When word circulated around the school about my impending departure, it was Verna Peterson who sat with me to talk about my plans for the future. More importantly, she wanted me to care fervently about never losing my dreams. Other teachers, of course, expressed their "good-byes." Though they were graciously given, they never compared with the last lesson by Mrs. Peterson.

In retrospect, I do believe Verna Peterson's constancy of interest and positive regard gave me stability at a time when confusion, anxiety, and fear caused me to doubt all that I was. In retrospect, I do believe I lost a teacher, a mentor, a special friend, when I left her presence.

The other Peterson noted was the "yang" of the duo. I think of that part of the symbol as a somewhat forbidding element for me. Norma Peterson believed in being firm, demanding, and suspicious of the endeavors of all her students, especially those of her advisees. I was one of those students, one of those advisees.

Four years after leaving the large public high school, after attending a private boarding school for girls, after graduating in 1962, I enrolled in college as a history major. What happened to the "be a physician" dream? During my senior year at the boarding school, I was urged to turn my attention to the social sciences. I was strongly advised that it would be more suitable for me to set aside my interest in the physical sciences, especially medicine. Suitable, in this instance, meant parental doubt and disapproval of my earlier desires. The decision was a simple one—one imposed by them.

What followed at the Fall Freshman Convocation held during the first week of college altered my life. I learned I was to be an advisee of Dr. Norma Peterson, the imposing professor of history, and the chair of the Social Science Division. During the convocation, most of the speeches which explained the focus and goals of each college division were at best unexciting. However, when Peterson spoke, all attention focused on her words—especially those regarding the kind of students she would allow into the Social Science Division. In a formidable manner, she stated that her division, her department wanted only students willing to work and to work hard. There would be no tolerance for laggards. Somehow I felt challenged by her words. Sitting there that day, I was proud that I was to be her student. Sitting there that day, I was terrified that I was to be her student. Those two emotions—pride and fear—held sway for the duration of my undergraduate years as Peterson dictated my education in history, Latin, German, and geology. I was told exactly what courses to take and when to take them. I did so.

Warmth is not an adjective I would use to describe Professor Peterson. She carried herself with an austere military-like bearing, with her saber-like knowledge at the ready to slice down students who did not do her bidding. We students had to "like" doing her bidding. Peterson knew exactly what she wanted us to be. Scholars. And, no matter the field of study at this juncture in my life, I wanted acceptance as an excellent student. Did I want to be a scholar for her? Yes. I wanted that saber to touch my shoulders and knight me as a chosen one.

Angst of not being a chosen one ruled my emotions at some point every day. If Prof. Peterson did not nod or speak to me as we passed in a hallway, I felt devastated. Every historical fiber in me knew that I was being rejected. To me, the perceived rejection meant more than fear of receiving lower grades, it meant I was not worthy of being acknowledged. Non-acknowledgement had always plagued me in my home life. Thus, from this professor, I wanted, needed to be acknowledged in a positive manner.

I, and other history majors, set Peterson on a professorial pedestal. She had a Ph.D.—a Doctor of Philosophy in History. She taught in higher education. By implication, she expected us to follow the course she had set, to do the same as she had done. Was I impressed by Peterson's credentials? Oh, yes. Did she and her aura further impel me to forgo medical studies? Oh, yes. So, I stifled, I crushed the old desire that another Peterson had once nurtured. Obtaining a Ph.D.—in history—became my goal. Teaching at a university drew my focus. I became a "Peterson- Student."

However, the time under the professor's tutelage was fraught again and again with tension, even distress. Every Peterson course required a lengthy research paper. For one such paper, I chose to compare and contrast the thoughts, philosophies, and writings of Erasmus and Thomas More. And, I was proud of my research and writing, particularly of original segments assessing the correspondence between those Renaissance scholars. At the grading interview, Peterson initially made bland comments about my observations. Then, the saber cut into the paper. She red-inked, figuratively bloodied, the portion of the study in which I had made my creative statements. She glared at me, and asked from what source I "copied" the words. Stunned is too mild a word to describe my reaction. I sat frozen in that severe wooden armchair by her desk. I had been accused of plagiarism—the death knell for a student. Then, I tried to search for words, to defend my work. And, what was Peterson's icy response? She said she did not believe me, even though she had herself searched to find sources with "my words" in them. In a demeaning manner, Peterson allowed that the paper showed good "basic" writing skills. Yet, she so doubted my assertions that she just had to give the paper—and me—a "C-minus" grade.

Why did I remain in Peterson's clutches? I simply, desperately, needed her approval—the approval of another authority figure. Other department professors praised my endeavors in Medieval and Modern European history, and in German and Latin. Had Peterson and my parents assented, I might have studied in freedom at Heidelberg University in Germany. But, the hope I had never trumped the influence to keep me from such study. Her desire to have me follow her plans seemed too controlling. The patterns of behavior almost mirrored actions I saw in other areas of my life.

I must say that Peterson's lectures, during which each student took copious notes, could be rewarding. Her observations about the magnificent playwright Eugene O'Neill were among the best ones I ever heard. Ironically, it may have been such lectures which helped me explore a new world of experiences in the realms of theatre. I was a total novice, but one winter evening, I happened to audition and gain a role in the play about Sir Thomas More, the heroically tragic figure about whom I had written the "C-minus" paper. I gained inner-strength as More's wife in "A Man for All Seasons." Following that theatrical excursion, I ignored Peterson's standard, imposed directives, carried an overload, and enrolled in two courses in oral interpretation of literature. I had found a new kind of acceptance. And,

I incurred Peterson's everlasting enmity for my "frivolity." I had violated her high-minded academic rules. Her behavior toward me and my mixed feelings about that ran parallel to the behavior of my parents. There was always ample room for confusion.

After acquiring the Bachelor's Degree—in history, I turned away from Norma Peterson's hold to take on work to acquire a Master's Degree—in theatre. On graduation day for that latter degree, as I walked across the dais to receive my diploma and hood, my professors smiled with kind, gracious, approval. Except for one. From Peterson, there was only an angry, stony glare of disapproval.

I do consider and reflect with care about the effects on me during the years with the two Petersons. For both, I studied and acquired a solid academic education. From both, I learned much about the course, the direction a life may take. Now, I clearly see the yin and the yang—the white and the black— of the time under the influence of those two people. In the white years were care and shared hope. In the black years were anxiety and lonely fear.

There was Peterson. And, there was Peterson.

There was a glimpse of elation. There was a time of loss.
There was a need of new vision.

They Accepted My Proposal?

The academic fields of Communication Theory and Rhetoric were the focus of my doctoral studies in the early 1980s, and I admired, even loved, the thought in both. The latter area has existed for centuries. "The Rhetoric" written by Aristotle, and the earlier observations by Egyptians, played a wonderfully significant role in creating and establishing study of forms of language. In the 20th century, the distinguished theorist Kenneth Burke asserted in "A Grammar of Motives" that the function of language was to influence the communication through the use of symbols. All the works of Aristotle, Burke, and so many other theorists, I believed, should be combined in a broad field of study embraced by the term Communication Theory. Thus, rhetorical studies and areas such as Symbolic Interaction, Mechanism, Coordinated Management of Meaning—the list goes on—became part of my use of the umbrella term.

When the prolific writings presented in journal articles were in need of close, intense scrutiny, graduate communication programs enveloped them. At a number of universities in the United States, the communication theory course usually analyzed ten or twelve present-day research studies on elements of communication in our lives. The one or two textbooks which supplemented lectures and discussions presented the theories in complex, often obtuse, words and thoughts. Conclusions of the assertions sometimes left more questions unanswered, than answered.

Following the direction of graduate programs and courses, a movement began in numerous communication departments. Undergraduate students were to enroll in newly-offered theory courses. Only too soon, it became apparent that existing graduate communication theory textbooks were inappropriate, even for juniors and seniors. These undergraduates found it extremely difficult to fully grasp the bewildering language tenets, often quantitative, presented in the graduate-school-oriented textbooks.

The need to offer a communication theory course, especially for students proceeding toward advanced degrees, prompted me to urge our Department of Communication Arts at Ohio Northern University to include the course in our curriculum. I was excited about offering the course; however, I met the same problems faced by other professors across the country. Trying to use the available textbooks made students feel as if they were failures, that the material was "out in left field." Resentment grew. To counter that, I began to approach communication theory in ways more conducive to my students' interests. Their daily activities, their use of language became the focus of the concepts. Meeting people, forming relationships, reading eye contact, assessing symbols—these and so many more communication events from the past to the present provided a sense of personal reality for the students. "First-run" films they had never viewed supplemented understanding of the theories. The showing of "Nell," a film with Jodi Foster, brought a new light to the study of Symbolic Interactionism. I was always pleased when students could apply the contents of a film, such as "On Golden Pond," to a particular concept. Nonverbal Communication was delightfully received when they connected with "Tootsie." Such application of material produced a new world-view of communication for them.

I still searched for an acceptable textbook for the course. Each time a publisher's representative dropped by the office, the answer to my query was, "Sorry, none are on the market." One dull, gray, cold January day, as I again recited my tale of woe, one publisher's representative who was a rather intense, persuasive gentleman, interrupted, "Good grief, Roberts. Why don't you just write the text yourself?" "Thanks for the thought, but I don't think I'm good enough for that." "What do you mean by... not good enough? You're already using your own course notes like a book. You've got an outline. You've got the content...." He was on a roll with his perceptions.

That conversation began my relatively short saga as a textbook author. I tentatively agreed to think about the idea. Within a week, the firm sent an entire packet of publishing information. It was voluminous. My anxiety grew exponentially as I read and re-read all the criteria for submitting a book proposal. I would have to develop a table of contents, structure a book outline, write several model chapters, include an examination of all existing communication theory texts and related material, and present a definitive need for my type of textbook. Frankly, all I could do was to tell myself "Don't do this." I was overwhelmed as I considered approaching such an intimidating task. I also felt it could be more than a little embarrassing if the editor and his staff refused the proposal for my textbook. Yet, I felt a need, a need to try to write the proposal, and eventually the book.

So, I did try. First, I analyzed books and materials even vaguely related to communication theory. Then, I provided outside reviews of each. I developed a probable table of contents, and outlined the book and each of the potential chapters. Developing the bibliography for the book proposal presented some difficulty. Fewer sources were available than I first thought. I always had an enjoyable penchant for bibliographic searches; however, finding material was a disappointing struggle.

Introducing theories that had never been presented or theories that had been given only passing recognition in existing communication theory texts was a major part of my plan. It appeared that most theoretical studies were based on quantitative analyses. I wanted to add qualitative material. Contrary to custom, I chose to include material on rhetoric—its foundation, development, and current thought. At the time of my work, rhetoric as a field of study itself owned a multitude of writings from the ancient Greeks— consider Aristotle's scholarly, wide-ranging achievements. The intervening centuries, and especially the years of the 20th century, also provided a significant number of achievements by fine rhetoricians.

As if that inclusion of rhetoric wasn't heretical enough, I wanted to begin each chapter's topic with a narrative presented in such a fashion as to "draw in" the students' interest. The following segment was a portion of the Introduction to the proposed textbook:

"Imagine a frost-cold morning, just past a very ancient dawn 15,000 years ago. You and other men, women, and children seek comfort around ftres at the mouths of caves you call home. You pull your fur pelt around you for more warmth, and walk toward a cave entrance slightly apart from the others. The flame of the torch you carry wavers and sputters in the gusts of air emerging from the black portal. You shiver, then proceed half- sliding, half-stumbling across a damp, dirt surface. Once past the entry rocks, you turn and with the glowing

torchlight you experience a wall of vivid colors—yellows, blacks, browns, reds, whites. Before you are re- creations of beings you know so well—individual animals drawn with magniftcent strokes, portrayed with grace of movement and sophistication. You advance further into the darkness and enter other inner caverns with depictions of symbols, people, and other animals—imposing stags, lumbering bison, huge bulls. These paintings, these inscriptions leave you with a sense of great wonder and awe, just as they will do so for the young boys who will discover them on a warm September day in 1940, near Lascaux, France. But why did the members of your clan, those people who taught you to seek out the great mammoth, come down into these dark caverns and bequeath their marks for all time? You know, for you entered the place of mystery to learn of rituals and totems. You and others like you learned your lessons well—you learned to believe. And, that is the gift of the ancient ones to us many decades, many epochs apart. With your positively elegant forms, you communicated belief. You… communicated.

These ancient ones spoke to one another and have spoken across the centuries to each one of us. They communicated with us who still wear fur pelts against the morning chill, and carry forms of torches to light our way in the darkness. It is a marvelous word—"Communication." Yet, as remarkable as it is, this oft-used term can be a most difficult one to deftne and understand. Although we may not be able to develop one precise, all-purpose, handy-for-every-job deftnition of communication, our study can yield a better understanding of myriad ramiftcations and concepts surrounding the term.

Let us begin with the most accessible tools to use in embarking on your modern study of communication. You may go to any number of dictionaries in any number of libraries, or even pick up the one you brought to school. It's the one that's a bit dusty up on the top shelf of your bookcase. You may open the provocative pages, and expose to the light of day a signiftcant number of interpretations of communication...."

I assembled such narratives and their chapters, along with the other required material, and sent the proposal to the communication editor. Within one month, Martin, representing the company, called to set up a meeting to discuss the book proposal. So, on a warm February day, he arrived to take me to a fine lunch at a rather charming little restaurant near the university. If my anticipation was high for the meal, it was off the scale regarding what he would say about the textbook proposal. My thoughts were not exactly positive. Vision after vision of "We're sorry, but..." passed through my mind as cordial chit-chat occupied our meal. Then, Martin slowly brought out a large file from his briefcase. "Our publishers have a few pages they want you to read carefully and to sign. It's a contract, you see. And,... they'd like you to accept a $1,000-advance on your project." I was silent for a moment, then, in a dumbfounded way, hesitantly asked, "Does that mean... does that mean they accepted my proposal?" He chuckled. "The proposal, yes. And, they look forward to accepting your book. Our communication editor said that you should put to rest any doubts about your writing concerning this project." I began my venture as a book author that weekend, and every weekend after. Until the end of spring quarter in late May, those days were all I could give to the task. I still had to manage my schedule of daily classes with lectures, discussions, and grading. My friends were supportive, my students were supportive. Some people—nameless now—were frankly unsupportive. They simply thought I was not good enough to do such work. The last attitude hurt, but did not deter me from my writing. I was proud of my first chapter for this theory book which began with the communication, the rhetoric, of the ancient Egyptians and Greeks. Finally, there was to be a textbook of theory beginning at "the beginning."

After May graduation, I worked diligently day by day on the book's manuscript. The process of the research, planning, and writing phases was actually energizing. Completing each chapter and sending it to the editor brought more requests for more chapters. The editor wanted to advertise the text as an upcoming one in time for the annual meeting of the National Communication Association. However, this was not to be.

During the spring and summer as I wrote, I began to have difficulty seeing clearly. Frustration grew. About once per month, I needed new lenses for my glasses. Writing slowed and depression increased. I had to keep putting off requests to write and send more chapters. My thoughts were plagued by the old statements such as "I told you that you couldn't do it." or "You're not good enough for this." By November, I was totally unable to see. Work ceased on the book. Teaching became impossible, and the university generously granted a lengthy medical leave. The diagnosis of Fuchs Dystrophy, in which cells pumping fluid throughout the cornea die, and swelling results, had caused blindness in both eyes.

The only hope of ever regaining any vision would have to come through cornea transplants. Waiting—for transplants, for surgeries, and for year-long recoveries for each eye—became the norm. I found myself in a sit-and- listen-to-books-on-tape existence. I felt time creeping by. And, I knew it was doing the same for the publisher. After two years of struggle, the editor and I finally and sadly agreed to discontinue the writing project. My textbook was to have been a fresh entry into the market. Even regaining a modicum of sight following three transplants provided no impetus for me to renew the project. By that time, concepts I had openly shared had made their way into new undergraduate communication theory texts. Professors, who once had no resource, now had two or three available book choices.

Because the new textbooks with similar chapter introductions, topics, and organization, were well-received, completing and adding "my" book version would have appeared as a replication of them—and not as an original endeavor. There was some pleasure, though, in knowing that a number of my colleagues across the country continued to successfully use the unpublished drafts of my completed chapters in their own courses, just as I did in mine.

In recalling those years in my life, I can simply state that once I could see, then I could not see, then I could see again. I learned much during those times. And, despite all the adversity, I have never stopped loving language-words- symbols. They bring to us visions of our world.

University professors are often accused of living in an "ivory tower," oblivious of other elements of society—elements that do not wear flowing robes and draped hoods for ceremonial occasions. In an endeavor to rectify the negative perception, five professors from Ohio Northern University ventured forth to participate in a non-ivory tower event. Perhaps they desired to see if Julius Caesar's oft-repeated "Veni. Vidi. Vici." assessment of his military excursions in Gaul would apply to their new fall excursion in Ohio.

Knives, Guns, Dogs… and Lawn Tractors

Labor Day. Nine-o'clock a.m. Five chuckling professor-types stood admiring their attire. Old walking shoes. Worn blue-jeans. Baggy, long-sleeve shirts. Ball-caps. Western hats. Dr. Seuss' Cat-in-the-Hat top-hats. We were set to go. We inserted ourselves into a silver C-Class Mercedes. We agreed we had to "move it" in order to get a parking place before the gates opened.

We did move. Ten-o'clock a.m. We got there. We were directed by parking personnel to a spot in a huge hay- field. We exited the Mercedes. It looked lost among the RVs, SUVs, 4x4s, and Monster Trucks. We took deep breaths. We acted like we knew what we were doing. We crossed the two-lane country road. We paid $10.00 each to pass through a large rough-hewn, wooden gate. We paused. We had arrived—for the National Coon-Dog Trials and Festival.

The Coon-Dog Trials were held each Labor Day weekend in fields and forests southwest of Kenton, Ohio. The four-day event drew thousands of interested—and interesting—individuals from all the adjoining states, and well- beyond. These folk came as if drawn by unseen forces to compete, to sell, to buy, to simply observe. The grounds of the encampment consisted of row-after-row of tables, booths, tents, and pavilion-like set-ups. Blinking holiday lights, Japanese paper lanterns, and myriad-size flags caught the attention of customers-to-be. To a "T," every seller had red-white-and-blue American flags hung from poles of varying heights.

Typical and not-so-typical flea-market booths offered such items as long, multi-colored, heavy, wool scarves. These sold out early during the Festival, despite the humid 92-degree temperature. Crocheted, beaded doilies were available to buyers as potential "Birthday gifts, Christmas gifts, Presidents' Day gifts, Independence Day gifts, and Thanksgiving Day gifts," so the vendor's sign politely stated. "Genuine" crystal vases and bowls attracted much interest, as did odd-numbered sets of old Fiesta-ware dishes. A sea of men's, women's, and children's white socks (8- pair for $1.00, thank you) occupied numerous spaces. But, by far and away, the biggest-selling products, found at every booth and in every tent, were T-shirts for infants, toddlers, pre-teen-agers, teen-agers, twenty-to-thirty something-agers, middle agers, and the —agers beyond counting-years. All the rainbow colors could be seen. However, certain ones—the best and most popular—sold out ever so quickly. These T-shirts were immediately put on and worn during all the days of the huge event. Each expressed opinions or inclinations. There were T-shirts emblazoned with dire consequences for anyone who violated personal property; T-shirts expressing love of god, guns, and women; plus, T-shirts sporting citations of Second Amendment rights.

Other velvet-draped tables, colorful booths, and canvass tents focused on the visitors' intrigue with blades. The entries took the forms of cutlery sets, jack-knives, pocket-knives, pen-knives, and switchblades. Some vendors displayed, exchanged, and sold replicas of the famous Bowie knife, complete with a fifteen-minute narrative about it creator. Bayonets, trench knives, and daggers accompanied tales of combat, as did halberds, and tomahawks. Work implements such as hatchets, axes, and cleavers drew attention, along with historic sabers, rapiers, foils, scimitars, lances, spears, and striking imitations of King Arthur's Excalibur. The historian in our academic group tried to engage the sellers with her own "accurate" interpretations about many of the weapons' various uses. However, her comments regarding the instruments of destruction just couldn't compete with the florid, garish accounts of the weaponry, as told by the booths' authorities who were more bent on making profits.

The variety of assorted blades held considerable interest as visitors strolled the wide, grassy paths of the flea- market. However, some areas had so many people gathered together that we had to elbow our way to get through the crowd and see the wares. There, on tables, and hanging from peg-boards, were guns—guns to be examined, guns to be sold, guns to be traded. Men and women openly sported their guns as they sought out like souls with whom they haggled about gun-quality, and prices.

The assortment of firearms was phenomenal. Sellers and buyers had access to all types of guns. Brand names were bandied about, as we heard references to Colt-45s, Glocks, and Lugers. There was an incredible amount of intense discussion as the attendees—the hunters and the curious— noted attributes, judged the strengths and weaknesses, and declared the necessity of owning and using pistols, revolvers, repeaters, automatics, even derringers. Descriptions of some guns as shooting-irons, six-shooters, side-arms, and rods belied aged-experience. There was talk about pieces, heaters, enforcers, single and double-barrel shotguns, and even sawed-off shotguns reminiscent of the "Bonnie and Clyde" era. Some old history buffs fancied the likes of muskets, breechloaders, flintlocks, and dare one say, a blunderbuss or two.

Passing through, stopping with the crowds, and learning far more about knives and guns than we could have imagined were definite features of the day. However, one highlight of our little adventure was observing the behavior of dogs. Some walked passively by, firmly leashed by their owners and handlers. Other dogs were in large pens, complete with protective housing. "Going to the dogs" literally meant walking around enclave after enclosure situated in the shade of the large trees on the acreage.

There were no mutts at this affair. The dogs, dogs, and dogs were highly-bred canines. The barking and baying could have come only from hounds. And, these were not the caricature hounds with slobbery jowls. Bloodhounds were in evidence; but, we soon learned about the "real" hounds—coon hounds. Red-ticks, and Blue-ticks with their distinctive reddish-brown, and blue-black spots dominated the offerings. These dogs were hunters-of-raccoons, and relished the activity of "treeing a coon." The dogs tracked and chased the dark-gray critters with bushy, ringed tails. The object of numerous contests, held during the nights at the Festival, was to "set" the hounds to find a raccoon which had climbed to the safety of the branches of trees. Once the coon-dog accomplished that, it began to bay to indicate its position to the hunter-owner. The awards went to the dogs who found and "tree-ed" their prey first. We were relieved to learn that no actual raccoons were injured or killed during the contests. A smelly piece of "bait" had been placed in the trees before each round began.

One rather exciting sport involved dogs that had been taught to leap as far as possible into a long pool of water to retrieve a thrown object, imitating the actual retrieval of waterfowl that had been shot. The dog which leaped the farthest became the event champion, after qualifying, semi-final, and final leaps. The cheers, heard a quarter-mile away, brought us to that contest trial. And, like most observers, we began to place bets on our favorite dogs. As amateurs, we chose mainly good-looking, friendly-looking dogs. Such gambling came close to decimating our pocket stashes. By the time we had but a few dollars left, we happily served as part of the cheering, whistling gallery.

There were two reasons for our limited funds. The first reason we never could recall. The second reason we did recall. Shortly after entering the Festival grounds, we purchased large bags of popcorn. Then, to quench our thirst, we bought beer, but not in cans. Use of cans was decidedly frowned on. Use of plastic half-gallon or gallon jugs was *de rigueur* for the day. We took our gallon container, filled with Bud-Lite, and poured the golden essence into five, tall, red plastic cups. Stations for replenishing the jugs were strategically located for strollers such as our group. Large public restrooms were also strategically located nearby. We neophytes to the event did not exactly get drunk; however, we complained less and less about the dust and the heat, and admired more and more the flea-market offerings. Even the knives and guns appeared promising, as we spoke about them, using our newly acquired knowledge.

After filling our cups one last time, having purchased far too many gallons of suds, we decided to head in different directions to view more areas of interest. But, we did agree to meet at the covered, picnic pavilion about 4- o'clock for pulled-pork sandwiches and coleslaw, all prepared by the local church ladies from Kenton. Two of us headed toward the chain-link fence which surrounded the Festival grounds. We acquired two grassy spots, and sort of slid down the fence, in order to "rest-a-bit." Then, we saw the parade—or what we thought was a parade— without marching bands. Coming closer to our personal viewing section, was a dust-covered, green, John Deere lawn tractor, driven by a cheery fellow in a Santa suit. The diminutive tractor pulled an eight-foot-long flatbed trailer. On said trailer were two, beat-up sofas decorated with red bunting and green helium balloons. Sort of sitting and draped on the sofas were ladies of varying dimensions, small and large, mostly large. As they and their equipment passed by, heading who knows where, the sofa occupants tossed packages of red-and-green chocolate candies to the whistling, cat-calling audiences.

The two of us looked at each other, looked at our beer cups, shook our heads, took one last gulp, and poured the leftover elixir into the grass. We tried to stand, then sank down to our grassy spots, as the next lawn tractor, cum trailer, came into view. This time, someone chomping on a long cigar, dressed in a blue, bunny-suit, steering his bright yellow, Cub Cadet lawn tractor, guided another trailer down the path. Seated, and tipping precariously, on black, metal, folding-chairs were more ladies wearing something akin to versions of Playboy-bunny costumes. These ladies might have been considered "ladies-of-the-evening," however, the sun was shining brightly and the humid temperature was now 96-degrees. As the occupants passed by, they gave out only sweet smiles and generous wiggles of their tails. We knew, at that moment, it was definitely time for a pulled-pork sandwich.

When we five finally gathered together, the doubting-threesome laughed and made wise-cracking remarks about our tale of the seasonal parade. They also cited our beer consumption as cause for our hallucinations. Their disbelief turned to amazed credence as a vivid red, International Harvester lawn tractor driven by an Uncle Sam, passed by the pavilion. Flags, appropriately American, and a few scantily-clad, lady-soldiers, carrying honest-to-god guns, decorated the accompanying trailer. We didn't know whether to stand and salute, or just sit in amazement. After that patriotic vision, we five decided that it was, indeed, time to return to the Mercedes, which we assured ourselves would not have a flatbed trailer attached. After a minor bit of searching, we found the Mercedes, and slowly and gently creaked our way into the car. All the strolling had taken a toll. A sort of thoughtful silence pervaded as we drove from our grassy field, and headed home.

Labor Day. Six-o'clock p.m. Five academic-types seemed to contemplate, to meditate even. Thence, busy discussion and questioning ensued. Had we really encountered what we thought we saw? Yes, there had been a flea-market. Yes, there had been knives. Yes, there had been guns. Yes, there had been dogs. And finally, yes, and yes again, there had been lawn tractors. Nothing else in our scholarly world of experiences could compare. We had come. We had seen. We had conquered, or rather survived, the National Coon-Dog Trials and Festival.

In May, with dogwood, forsythia, redbud in bloom, I saw tragedy.
I saw evil. I saw a country at war with itself.
I wished to close my eyes and not see the truth. I could not.

One Small Measure

A man gave commands that day.

He was an angry, old leader; the guardsmen were confused, young followers. He was weary and hated protests; the soldiers were tired and feared protests.

One-nine-seven-zero.

He zeroed in on Kent State, the soldiers zeroed in on students.

Hurtful words-ugly shouts-raised M-1s.

Thirteen seconds-sixty bullets-piercing screams.

Eleven wounds-four deaths.

Jeffrey and Allison and Sandra and William.

He snarled of brown-shirts, communists, night-riders.

He washed his hierarchical-plate clean of blame.

Simple, confused outrage became complex, focused fury.

College and College and College closed.

University and University and University closed.

Flushed with fear, flushed with anger, flushed with purpose beyond:
"What did we learn in class today?"
Protests were planned, marches were formed.
A nation held its collective breath.

Students looked east, looked east at perceived corruption,
Looked east toward the Washington Temple granting slaughter half-a-world away.
That May night, young and earnest youth came to our tree-green, stately-Gothic, college campus.

In our place of learning, we gave pens, papers, phones to help say the war must stop. In our haven of safety, we showed our care, our sadness, our dismay.
Student and teacher, the young and the old, reached toward one another.

Then came a pause in the flurried activity.
In that dark night, in that dark time, in that moment,
There was silence.
And, one small measure of peace.

THE STUDENT DIMENSION

An atypical way of addressing a university professor became my moniker.
Its use identified me in such a way that students did not resort to the overly
familiar, "Elizabeth," nor the overly formal, "Professor Roberts, ma'am."

Hey, Lady… !

"Hey, Lady! Let's get Girt, the Dirt, on the move. We've got a plane to catch!"
And, indeed, we did. "Hey, Lady! Going to Parkersburg is like going to early
Nationals!" And, indeed, it was. "Hey, Lady! Do you mean we're going to
stay on the Canadian side of The Falls?" And, indeed, we were.

In 1973, as I began my teaching career at Ohio Northern University,
I was assigned to coach the Individual Events Speech Team. Unlike team
debating, I. E. focused on informative, sales, persuasive, impromptu, and
extemporaneous speaking. I. E. also embraced oral interpretation of prose,
poetry, and drama selections. I initially felt overwhelmed by the task of
coaching students for competition in these areas of speaking. In Ohio,
the speech tournaments were regarded as some of the most difficult in
all the Midwest. In addition, students from colleges and universities in
surrounding states—Michigan, Pennsylvania, West Virginia, Kentucky,
and Indiana— competed for the excellent speaking experiences with the
hope, of course, of obtaining trophies for their endeavors.

The tournaments could be grueling, especially for students who chose
to participate in two or three events. On a Friday, Saturday, and Sunday,
students competed in elimination rounds, quarter-finals, semi-finals,
and the top-of- the-line finals. While the president or dean of the host

institution warmly and graciously welcomed the competitors, the students spent their time "scoping" their rivals. "Look at the size of those extemp. case notes." "Oh, god, the O.U. drama-duo team is here again."

There always was a semi-pretended interest in the style of the trophies which were usually displayed in the front of the school's theatre where the students were welcomed. Most trophies were beautifully-inscribed, walnut-based, brass figures or goblets. At one tournament hosted by Hope College in Holland, Michigan, Trish, an informative speech competitor, noted that there were trophies for only the first, second, and third-place winners in each category, and these trophies were inscribed, colorfully decorated, wooden shoes. Those shoes represented the wonderful tulip festival being hosted by this U.S. "Holland." It was not that the trophies were wooden shoes that bothered her. It was that there were only three pairs for the top three finalists in each speech division. She noted for the umpteenth time, "Lady, there should be a pair for each final place, or, maybe, one shoe for each of the six places." The rest of our team grumbled, sort of, at her questionable inappropriate attitude; however, some of those same contestants also felt a bit like Trish.

AlthoughTrish's Informative Speech on the non-verbal "Bubble of Personal Space" had been a winner at four previous competitions, this time she had unfounded doubts. However, Trish did achieve top places in all of the qualifying rounds and did become one of six finalists. At the award ceremony, the winners in all categories were slowly announced proceeding from third place to first. When the tournament director came to Informative Speaking, "Third" went to a student from Hope College, "Second" to a student from Ohio University, "First" to… there was a pause. Trish looked crushed. She just knew she had been in the bottom third of the finalists. Then, she realized that her name and that of Ohio Northern University, were announced. I had never seen such a thrilled young woman. Her talent was once again affirmed, as was that of ONU's new entrants, Marcy and Peg in drama- duo, Carol in sales speaking, and Charles in impromptu speaking. There were wooden shoes all over the place, so to speak. Each student's achievement remained a delightful hallmark for me. On the trip back to Ohio in the our orange and black ONU van, Trish remarked, "I think that having a pair of engraved wooden shoes in this striking blue lettering is far superior over having just one shoe." The team and I almost throttled her.

Pride and joy for all the team members were wonderful emotions to feel after each competition, each month, each year. As a coach, I was obligated to judge round after round of multiple presentations. A fifty-minute round would end, I'd complete the assessment forms, take them to the judging room, and rush, even run on to another event in another room, or building. Exhaustion captured not only the students, but also one very tired coach. However, as a "reward" for all their exceptional endeavors, I'd take them to a fine restaurant for an even finer meal the last evening of the competition. ONU's team became the envy of many schools. Ohio Northern's administration admired the students' work and the credit that our school received. It saw no restraint in treating them to a lovely repast—steak, seafood, pasta. In Athens, Ohio, the students voted for the "Oak Room;" in Columbus, Ohio, it was the "Victoria Station;" in Parkersburg, West Virginia, there was no question that the "Point of View" would be the choice. This elegant restaurant was on a high bluff overlooking historic Blennerhasset Island in the middle of the Ohio River. Our position at the north-facing windows offered an incredible view of blinking lights and moaning horns of river boats and barges wending their way in the expansive black ribbon of water.

Depending on the number of ONU competitors, we would all pile into my Dodge Dart—"Girt-the-Dirt," or into one of ONU's vans painted the school colors of orange and black—"The Noble-Mobile-Pumpkin." Late one spring, ONU sent five students and me to George Mason University in Fairfax, Virginia, located just outside of Washington, D.C. Carol, Beth, Rob, Charles, and J. B. had never flown. As we left ONU, Girt-the-Dirt was colorfully decorated for "The Ducks" luck. The Debate Team—"The Turkeys"—had wished us well. Girt-the-Dirt provided an amazing sight with balloons and posters flapping in the wind current, as we drove south on I-75 to Dayton, Ohio. Once on our American Airlines flight, the team fairly glowed with surprise when a flight attendant welcomed the Ohio Northern University Speech Team and wished the students success on their journey.

In that dark night, the plane passed over the middle of Ohio. J. B., a young fellow from southern Ohio's city of Gallipolis, where his strong speech accent was like that found in Kentucky, turned his interest to Carol who sat next to him in the window seat. "Lookee ther Carol, we's passin' yer house, 'n' there's yer mom a wavin' a yeller flashlight at us'ns." Carol quickly turned to look out the window, then, sheepishly realized J. B. had "got her"—especially with his exaggerated accent. She finally did give in to the infectious laughter of the team and all the surrounding passengers.

The wonderful historic sights of Washington rivaled the excitement of the tournament. The students garnered trophies but they also garnered a special appreciation for the Capitol and the Supreme Court. The Lincoln, Washington, and Jefferson memorials brought a subtle sensitivity. There were open tears at the Viet Nam Memorial. Awe and inspiration engulfed them at the Smithsonian, as they observed the decades of growth from Wilber and Orville Wright's airplane to John Glenn's space capsule. Our tours of the city brought confusion and laughter as our rental car went round and round roundabouts, and tried to follow the alphabet soup of streets, avenues, and boulevards. We kept switching drivers, but to no avail. Finding food sources was no problem. Getting five disparate appetites to agree on one restaurant choice was the problem.

Two years later, our Speech and Theatre Department, with additional funds from then President Samuel L. Meyer, sent two debaters and one informative speech contestant to another Washington, and the Pi Kappa Delta Speech Fraternity National Tournament in Seattle. Once again, it was a first flight for Joseph, Pete, and Trish, and once again there was a welcome from American Airlines. Walking trips up and down the hills and around the beautiful flowering city and its noted Pike Street Market caught all kinds of attention. An additional special interest was a ferry trip across the dark inlet to Blake Island for smoked Pacific Sockeye Salmon, and fantastic feather dances by members of Inuit tribes.

The students on the speech teams always had a sense of gracious appreciation for their travels and experiences subsidized by ONU. However, Joseph, Pete, and Trish wanted to show a special "Thank You" to President Meyer. They knew he had countless polar bear pictures, paintings, and sculptures. And, they wanted desperately to add to his collection of ONU's mascots a gift from the Pacific Northwest. For these students, costs for sculptures were prohibitive. However, on one rather windy walk up and down Seattle's famous streets, a shop that sold scrimshaw beckoned their interest. There in an old oak and glass case was their treasure to be—a scrimshaw polar bear tie-tack. Together they voiced their concerns: "Do you think Dr. Meyer already has one?" "I hope not." "I've never seen him with one on." "Let's get it guys—this is one unique bear!" They took that chance.

When the threesome returned, they were called in officially for an interview with President Meyer to "discuss" the Seattle excursion. So, complete with their best attire, and the awards, they entered the "inner sanctum." President Meyer could not have been more gracious. However, once the three contenders were seated he began: "Joseph and Pete, just what strategy did you use for your topic? What kind of research helped? What was the competition like? And, Trish, do you think your judges learned new information from your Practice of Pharmacy speech? Probably, your other competitors learned a lot, too?" Dr. Meyer, an old debater and speech competitor himself, knew just what to ask the team. Then, as he was thanking them for a fine representation of ONU, the trio interrupted him. "President Meyer, we want to show our appreciation for this trip—and here is our special Thank You." The president slowly opened the simple oak box, took out the tie-tack, replaced his own with the beautiful, skillfully carved white bear and, with glistening tears, that imposing man came around his desk, not only to shake hands, but also to give each one his noted "bear hug." A few days later as our paths crossed on campus, President Meyer happily waved his tie. "See, Professor Roberts, I've got it on!" Now it was my turn for a few subtle tears.

In an academic department, there are always the achievers. And, then there are those who go one step beyond as super-achievers to assist professors and staff members as "go-fers." These students assembled faculty handbooks for courses, made countless treks in all kinds of Ohio weather to deliver vital messages and materials, and worked well beyond usual hours in the theatre scene shop. Marcy, Peg, and Carol epitomized such students, in addition to their academic and tournament achievements. The three young women had earned awards at numerous individual events competitions in sales, impromptu, and drama-duo categories. With all their first-place rankings, the three students qualified for a trip to a national competition. As a thank you for all their many accomplishments, the chair of our department advised, "Treat them well. Let's splurge on these young women who have given so much to us." I followed his directive. We drove "Girt-the-Dirt" to Buffalo, New York, and on toward the immense, incomparable Niagara Falls. The trio who thought we were just stopping for a brief view were overjoyed when we crossed the Rainbow Bridge to Canada, and arrived at a well-appointed Canadian hotel. In awe, Marcy said, "Let's forget the speeches and just stay here for three days!" "Too bad, ladies. That's not going to happen. We've one hour to get to the tournament to register for this championship affair. Come on, Girt's a waitin' to cross back over the river!"

In between and after grueling qualifying rounds, our quartet became tourists. We admired the river and falls from the Canadian side, put on special rain gear to go down behind the huge falls, and drove north for a walk through historic Fort Niagara. Every evening, we tried to find a new restaurant for dining. However, we seemed to find the Hof brau Haus and its weinerschnitzel a standing date. Following the award ceremony, after quarters-, semis-, and finals, we drove back to Canada with trophies in hand to begin the packing process for the trip home to Ohio the next morning.

At 5:30 p.m., I called out, "Let's head to the tower, to the Skylon, for a few souvenirs from the gift shop." "Aw, Lady, do we have to go." "Yes, we all go together on these jaunts." So, reluctantly they joined me to go to the Skylon. I putzed around the shop a bit, then said, "Well, I don't know about each of you, but I'm going to take the elevator up to the viewing room." "But, Lady, that will cost $5.00 each." "I know. But, I have four tickets and 6:00 dinner reservations. Would you care to join me in the ride up? And, please try to pick up your jaws." So, up we went, were seated for an incredible view of the Falls, and delighted in the elegantly served offerings for our dining pleasure. At the top of the Skylon, the restaurant slowly revolved in an hour's time permitting views of Toronto, Buffalo, and Niagara Falls. There were gasps of pleasure just as the lights came on to illuminate those Falls in a magnificent play of rainbow-colored brilliance.

That treatment was just what had been ordered for the young women. Sadly, we loaded "Girt" on Sunday morning. As we readied to depart, Marcy requested that we stop at one of the Niagara Falls' gift shops to see if she could find one last thing for her mother. "OK, don't take too long. We'll take a last look at the Falls." Marcy returned shortly and we were ready to head out. "Wait a minute, Lady. We have a memento of our trip for you." "Now, that's not necessary. After all, this is your trip." But, I did open the blue box which contained a strikingly designed, seven-inch-high, blue and green ceramic duck. "Lady, this represents our team—the ONU Ducks." "It's an incredibly perfect choice for all of you." It really was, and it would find a place with all the trophies on display at Ohio Northern. "Wait, Lady, there's one more thing. This is just for you." I shook my head in wonder, and I opened a beautiful gold box. Inside, resting on black velvet, was an oval, black-and-white Wedgewood ring—one with a Greek goddess in white robes standing at a white lectern. She leaned graciously over it as though in deep thought. "Look, the Lady's speechless for once!" What could I have said at that moment. Only tears came.

We finally assembled ourselves and drove toward Ohio, through Ontario, on the King's Highway. Nothing was said for many a mile. We were happy. We were exhausted. Only at Point Pelee almost half-way home, did our energy grow again with the ideas of telling about our extraordinary trip. I have always treasured that journey—and that ring. I still wear it for special occasions. The Greek goddess represents Marcy, Peg, and Carol—and my years with all the wonderful young men and women who gave me visions of happiness, and, yes, love.

*I have lived day after day, throughout sixty-plus years, with known
and unknown, spoken and unspoken, fear. However, I have a fantasy
that someday I will see my world—my life—in which there will
be no gut-wrenching fear, in which I will be "good enough."*

Kaleidoscope of Fantasy

I have his autograph. He signed my script for "Kaleidoscope of Fantasy."
I stood before him across the speakers' table. The time was late May,
1977. The place was Los Angeles, California. The occasion was the
International Technical Communication Conference. He was the guest
speaker at the opening session. He was not offended that I had approached
him. His manner was quiet, gentlemanly, assured. He was pleased that
there had been a production—a Readers Theatre production—of five of
his short stories.

Although he was to address the technical society in a few moments, he
allowed time to inquire about the nature of Readers Theatre and his short
stories—his beautifully written fantasies. I told him that Readers Theatre
involved the re-creation of literature in the minds of the audience. For my
production, I chose five of his stories, each of which I adapted for university
student actors. As individuals they created and read the portions of a story
which depicted their particular character. Together they re-created the
complete story. The audience attending the production heard the fantasy
stories read from scripts enclosed in notebooks. The scripts figuratively
represented a book from which the audience might have been reading.

He asked about the stories I had adapted for the production. I related the titles and order of presentation. He smiled broadly, then, asked, "Would you send me a copy of your program script?" I nodded affirmatively. "Thank you so very much," he added. Almost giddy, I returned to my seat as the conference speeches began.

Mr. Ray Bradbury had created the stories in that script. Mr. Ray Bradbury wanted to read my adaptations of the stories. Mr. Ray Bradbury carefully wrote his address to which I was to send the scripted stories.... I did not. I did not send the material to him.

My action or lack of action was caused by fear—by a deep-seated, deep-rooted fear. My script was not good enough. My work was not good enough.

My life was not good enough. So afraid was I of Mr. Bradbury's potential comments, criticism, rejection, I placed my autographed script in its notebook on a shelf in my office. There it remained until I moved from that office when I retired in 2003.

I have thought carefully in recent months about that paralyzing fear. So many aspects of the time I've lived formed that fear. I fight it even in 2014. "It" resulted from the mixed emotions I felt beginning at age four. I never knew if I was to be confronted with love, or hate, or anger, or, especially, non-acknowledgement that I even existed. Somehow care from a select number of teachers, professors, doctors helped hold my life together which resulted in a resiliency that permits me to not merely exist, but to live this day.

Yet, even with that fear, I realized success. I taught at Ohio Northern University, gained tenure, gained a Ph.D., gained a Full Professorship. During thirty years, I taught and cared deeply for my students. Directing a public speaking program, and teaching courses in communication theory, persuasion, oral interpretation of literature, and other subjects figured importantly in my career.

What marked that career as special to me were the Readers Theatre productions I created and directed. In addition to "Kaleidoscope of Fantasy," the program of Ray Bradbury stories, I adapted other short stories by Isaac Asimov for "And the Universe Ceased to Exist;" and by Stephen King for "Tales of Terror and Imagination." I also adapted plays such as "Something Unspoken" by Tennessee Williams. There were programs filled with pathos. There were programs filled with delight and humor such as "A Touch of Laughter" with Eudora Welty short stories, and "Good Evening," an adaptation of revue sketches by Dudley Moore, Peter Cook, and Alan Bennett. A compilation and adaptation of the works of Carl Sandburg formed a biography of mankind I titled "The Earth Rocked Me." One program, performed for the ONU faculty and student forum, was "Tell Me How the Story Ends." Again, this was a collection of prose, poetry, and drama selections which focused on good, bad, and non-communication.

The creation of the programs dictated choices and decisions regarding distribution of story character lines, cutting of words and phrases, including or deleting "dialogue tags" and narration, yet always remaining faithful to each author's intent. Although the adaptation process for each story and program was often grueling, the result was rewarding for the student actors cast in the shows, the production staff members who assisted in mounting the shows, and the audiences who "lived" the stories. Yes, it was rewarding for me as the creator of the programs. Yes, it was rewarding for me as director of the programs. Yet, from proposal to the final lines of the last character, the fear of "It's not good enough." plagued me to my core.

Although fear always existed in me, somehow it did not hinder the "process" related earlier. I think I simply forged ahead. I do not know quite how I did it. Perhaps relating the development of one of the productions may provide a picture of what occurred with each Readers Theatre production. The following notes the inception and growth of "Kaleidoscope of Fantasy," which consisted of five short stories by Ray Bradbury.

For more than fifteen years, I had been an avid Bradbury fan. I, and many literary critics, chose to place his stories in the genre of "science fantasy" rather than science fiction as was the custom with many futuristic works. Bradbury's writings did not always occur in the "unknown future." Many pieces took place in "current time" and were beautiful imaginings. As I read and re-read Bradbury's stories, I thought that introducing them to a wider audience would be feasible through the interpretive form of Readers Theatre. Thus, with much trepidation, I took selected stories and formed them into character and narrative segments that became the script. Once accomplished, the set, lighting, sound, costume designers, and I met to plan the best way to present the adapted stories. Facility chosen: the octagonal-walled Elzay art gallery. Set design: two octagonal platforms, one on top of the other, in the center of the gallery with audience surrounding this "stage." Lighting design: instruments to spotlight or flood the stage area with colors from gold to blue to white. Sound design: excerpts from "The Planets" by Holst as recorded by the London Symphony Orchestra and as recorded electronically by Vangelis. Costume design: unisex dark brown slacks, dark brown turtlenecks draped in light tan flowing silk tops with bell-shaped sleeves. My anxiety level regarding these choices grew with each decision.

The "characters" in the stories were Ohio Northern University students who auditioned and were cast with the focus on vocal reading quality as individuals and in groups. The dedicated students were majoring in not only theatre, but also pharmacy, business, history, languages, engineering, music. The variety in majors became a casting custom in every Readers Theatre production.

With all the design elements in mind, I proceeded to "block" the stories with the selected readers. Each story required different placement of readers/ characters for maximum visual and vocal effect. Once done, rehearsals of the five stories began in earnest. Only four weeks had been allotted to prepare for performances. Movement, location, and lines were memorized. As is one custom in Readers Theatre, scripts were visible, bound in dark brown notebooks, to indicate the re-creation of the literature. Line rehearsals, movement rehearsals, technical rehearsals, and dress rehearsals all led to ushers opening the doors of the Elzay Art Gallery on a Thursday evening in early May, 1977. Soft symphonic music of "Venus," excerpted from "The Planets," greeted the audience. Then, with all the elements in place, the first performance began. In me, there was fear that the show would not be perfect.

The background music faded, the houselights faded, a blue glow lit the stage as four readers stepped onto the center octagon. The chilling mystery of "The Small Assassin" was unfolded by "the father," "the mother," "the doctor," and the narrator. The style of presentation, though unfamiliar, captured the attention of the audience. Because of audience seating around the stage, each member had a personal view of each story in the production.

Dimming of scene lights, subtle sounds from Holst, closing of notebooks, exiting of the four readers signaled the completion of "The

Small Assassin." Opposite actions brought the production to "The Off Season." Bright yellow light created the Martian desert on which the story occurs, with "Sam" and his hot-dog stand, "Elma" the cynical wife, and two blue-hooded readers for the Martian characters. Delightfully engaging, the story captured the audience and held them through the surprising, devastating ending. As before, lights dimmed, sound came up, the four readers exited smoothly as two more took places facing each other on opposite levels of the octagon. Stormy dark blue color brought to life "The Fog Horn." Characters of the young man and the old lighthouse keeper told the incredibly sad, dramatic vision of an ancient sea monster re-awakening and calling to the moan of the fog horn as though it were its lost mate.

The ending of the carefully orchestrated intermission began the fourth story, "Kaleidoscope." As the audience returned into the dimly red-lit art gallery/theatre, the electronic music version of "Mars, The War-Giver" began its heart-pounding crescendo. Seven male readers took places at the outer edge of the audience in the octagon corners. The music built and then "exploded." The gallery/theatre went totally black. A gasp of inhaled air came from the audience. Then the music cut to the "beep... beep... beep... beep" like that of a heart monitor. On the fourth "beep" and with each subsequent "beep," each reader, one-by-one, turned on a red-tipped pen-light. These readers were astronauts thrown, each alone, to the outer limits of the universe when their spaceship exploded. The pen-lights lit the script and the ghostly face of each reader. For the rest of Bradbury's merciless telling, the characters talked on the spacesuit mics until nothing was left but silence. As the dim red lights blinked out one-by-one, silence also overcame the audience.

A similar silence pervaded throughout the last selection, "And There Will Come Soft Rains." Five readers depicted a clock turning, rotating to its inexorable death in a fully automated futuristic house. The lighting was automatically set, the doors preset, dishes were cleaned, and little mice-like machines constantly ran around the house picking up all sorts of offensive material right down to lint. In the aftermath of a nuclear war, images of the children who were at play are burned into the walls of the automated house. Throughout the story, the clock keeps announcing the time, until it, too succumbs to the soft rains of total destruction. Icy lights down. House lights up.

I had only admiration for the artistic endeavors of the designers, the technical staff, and those devoted student readers. Together they had created a beautiful, intriguing production. The performances of "Kaleidoscope of Fantasy" captured each audience member in the worlds—the words—of Ray Bradbury. I had loved those words. I had not loved the fear. The fear of before, during, after. Someday—maybe—I will see no fear.

A glimpse of the experiences during my last academic quarter-
Winter, my last day-Friday, my last hour-2:00 p.m., before I retired
as a professor of communication arts at Ohio Northern University,
provides at least two reasons why the work of listening to 63,820
presentations over thirty-six years was totally rewarding.

Thank Y'all Vera, Vera Much!

Ethnic discrimination and political incorrectness in language use have long been a concern of mine in studying and teaching oral communication. What I listened to one day, however, could have violated every strongly held principle. On the one hand, the language I heard was typical of age-old "discrimination" about natives of the state of Kentucky by a native of the state of Ohio. On the other hand, the language I heard promoted what might be an object of dubious "correctness" for a gathering of both women and men. Where did I hear such language? In a university classroom. In a course in persuasive speaking.

Throughout the term of the course, the students, all juniors and seniors, and I discussed acquiring skills in receiving or being confronted with various forms of persuasive messages. We also approached and analyzed their responsibility to themselves and to society to create clear, positive, and ethical messages. Choice of messages, both written and oral, was a significant focus of the course. Thus, there were various types of assignments. There were impromptu speeches designed for students to think quickly and logically in order to devise and present a speech based on a quotation I selected. Each student had seven minutes in which to accomplish the task. There were also political speeches for or against a candidate for office or a representative party. Another type of speech was devoted to selling an activity or product. The students and I listened to sales presentations for everything from bicycles, to seven days on a cruise ship, to a wooden log that was not only a "toy" with character hats, but also an anatomically correct "doll" for health classes. An additional advantage, the speaker noted, was that the log could be burned in the fireplace once children were bored with this toy.

For the students' final speech in this persuasive speaking course, I gave them the task of convincing a hypothetical, medium-sized-community, library board either to retain or remove a magazine in the periodical section. The premise of the assignment was that the library was suffering a budget cut. Thus, the library needed to review proposed and existing periodicals. Each student with their magazine of choice was to focus on "pro" or "con" reasons for the addition, retention, or removal of said magazine. A list of criteria, which had to be addressed in the persuasive endeavor, included analysis of cover appeal, graphics, layout and design, letters to and responses from editors, advertisements, cost, and quality of articles. Each presentation was also to include the display of a copy of the chosen periodical.

In order to critique each speech, I chose to sit at a table in the back of the classroom. In an unobtrusive manner, I could scan the audience reactions, time the speeches, write comments, and observe each speaker's demeanor at the lectern. On the day for the presentations, I prepared the critique forms, grade sheets, stopwatch, pens, etc., as I usually did. I had not yet noticed what the student speakers were wearing nor what periodicals were selected.

"Gud aftanoon! Ahm so happa to be with y'all taday.... Me 'n' Jimmy, we jis moved 'ere from Kentucky, 'n' we'uns jis got oerselfs a bran' new double-wide 'n' parked it up at Northlan' Trailer Park 'ere in Ader, Ahia."

"Me 'n' Jimmy"... ? My head snapped up as I automatically clicked on the stopwatch and prepared to write comments about the opening of the speech. Bemused by the attire and dialect, I began to take in the persuasive phenomenon before me. I had asked for a volunteer to speak first. Jamie, sitting at the front table, had raised her hand. It should be noted that Jamie was an excellent student, a dean's scholar, a member of a distinguished national honor society, a member of Student Senate, and a member of other leadership organizations on the campus of Ohio Northern University. She was an attractive person, always conservatively and neatly attired. On this day, however, there at the lectern stood a young woman dressed in a black, tight-fitting, Harley Davidson t-shirt. Furthermore, her ensemble included a short, very short, black leather skirt, black fishnet stockings, and black calf-high boots. Her usually well-coifed hair was now accented by black, long, curly ringlets, large hoop-earrings, and heavy make-up with bright, very bright red lipstick. The *coup de grace* was a mouthful of chewing gum that rivaled any cud-chewing bovine.

"Me 'n' Jimmy sure wan' y'all to cum visit us!" She continued. *"But, y'all hafta git aroun' our two hogs in the front yard. Oh, them's the kinda hogs ya find on blocks.... Well, that brings me to why Ahm 'ere b'fore ya folk of this fine bookkeepin' buildin'. Me 'n' Jimmy want y'all to keep this 'ere Biker magazin' on yur shelfs."*

Complete with "cud-chewin," Jamie carefully covered the criteria for the presentation. The photos, articles, cost, all the elements as noted earlier, were addressed. However, the most persuasive moment came with Jamie's final appeal.

" Ya see, Jimmy—he don' read so gud. But, he cud cum to this 'ere bookkeepin' buildin' 'n' look at pichurs in Biker showin' how ta repair them there hogs of ours.... 'N' he cud fix 'em, 'n' then me 'n' Jimmy cud ride lak the win' ag'in!... Thank ya'll vera, vera much!"

After the laughter and appreciative applause subsided, a question arose for me. Did Jamie's unique presentation deserve an "A" as had all her other speeches in the course? Yes. Definitely, yes. The criteria had been met, and the speakin' and speaking skills were excellent in their creativity. Jamie, the biker, had thrown down the gauntlet. Thus, the other class members felt an obligation to "better" the "Biker" request. In the midst of all the competition, I tried to maintain a modicum of decorum. "Body Building," complete with assorted weights shown in the magazine, was a popular entry, as was "Sports Illustrated" cum balls, bats, gloves, and helmets. Recorded music accompanied the cleverly arranged speech for "Rolling Stone." More intellectual pursuits were represented by briefcase-toting speakers advocating for or against "The New Yorker," "The National Review," and "The Atlantic."

The final presentation, by Nate, offered a bookend to Jamie's "Hogs." Nate, also an excellent student and campus leader, was best known for his championship wrestling skills. His attire and demeanor were often rather laid-back- casual in denim jeans and white t-shirts. That last day, however, the pin-them-to-the-mat-competitor strode to the lectern dressed "to-the-nines" in a fine double-breasted, gray pin-stripe suit, a fine tailored light-blue dress shirt, a fine Windsor-knotted coordinating silk tie, and fine polished, black patent leather shoes.

Nate introduced, in an oh-so-professional manner, his magazine of choice—"Playboy." Not a few whistles and cat-calls greeted his introduction which began with a retrospective of prominent individuals who had been interviewed for the periodical. As Jamie and other class members had done, Nate thoroughly and conscientiously analyzed the magazine for its cost, letters, advertisements, graphics, and, of course, the excellent quality of the articles. The aspect of lay-out and design was presented as a double-entendre which served to heighten interest as we awaited the required display of the magazine. Prior to the unveiling, Nate offered an impassioned appeal to the imaginary library board, and asked for a positive decision to place the magazine on the periodical shelves.

As the moment for the critical revelation approached, I had no idea how I would critique the presentation, particularly the lay-out and design aspect of the "Playboy" centerfold. Should I stop Nate and take a moralistic high road, or just sigh and accept the inevitable? I sighed. The inevitable arrived. And, as if accompanied by ruffies and flourishes, Nate ever-so-slowly, ever-so-carefully opened "Playboy" to disclose the all-telling centerfold. There before us was the delectable beauty in all her glory—with all the pertinent parts covered by bright, very bright, yellow "Post-It-Notes." Nothing more could be said.

The speeches given by Jamie and Nate, and those by the other class members, provided a wonderful fitting end to the final class I taught at Ohio Northern University. During the days of this last persuasive speaking course, I had felt incredible pride and joy in listening to and seeing excellent, creative competition reign among the students. However, "Cud-Chewin" and "Post-It-Notes" will harbor special incomparable memories for years to come.

"Thank y'all vera, vera much!"

Our perceptions of ourselves can be so strongly chained to happenings in the negative past that we think we will forever be held captive by them. But, with hope, with beauty, and with love in the positive present, each link of that chain may weaken and crumble away. Then, we will be set free to claim a new vision.

The Earth Rocked Me

"I am more than a traveler out of nowhere..." Those definitive words of the noted Carl Sandburg began the final moments—the ending of a Readers Theatre production I had created, and which was presented at Ohio Northern University. It may seem odd to talk about the ending of a program when I should surely address my thoughts toward the actual beginning of what I called "The Earth Rocked Me"—a title from the poetic lines of Sandburg himself.

In years past, I had created other Readers Theatre productions, a style of theatre that takes prose, poetry, and drama selections, and weaves them orally in such a way that the voice, the words, the meaning of the literature is re- created in the minds of those listening, in the minds of the audience. With such events, minimal set, lighting, and costuming may provide only a minor physical suggestion. Matching black notebooks with the script—the words— carried by the readers/actors provide a mental suggestion. An audience member once approached me following a production and noted, "I could listen with my eyes closed, and see and feel the words. In a way, my parents could have been reading to me as we sat together on Sunday evenings sensing all in my mind's world."

As an outside-of-the-classroom activity, I set about to offer programs to ONU faculty, staff, students, and residents of the village of Ada. The productions, if examined for content, form an orchestral theme of my loves of varieties of literature never "staged" in any form.

There is always that "first one," the one that tugs at recalled emotions. Five stories by Ray Bradbury became a presentation of other-worldly fantasy. On and within octagonal platforms placed in an octagonal art gallery with the audience seated on all sides, "Kaleidoscope of Fantasy" found birth. The audience responded to the words with joy and laughter, with quizzical expression, and with not-so-unrealistic fear, as their minds met the crawling infant who killed its parents, the ancient sea-monster rising from the depths in love with the sound of the lighthouse horn, the mentally askew fellow who knew his hot-dog stand would profit wildly on Mars, the explosion of a space ship whose brave members talked as they were thrown to the nether regions of space, and the automated house still trying to function after a nuclear holocaust. Twelve aspiring readers brought all the adapted words to life, accented by symphonic and electronic pieces from Holst's "The Planets." A slight addendum: I met the engaging author of the short stories, Mr. Bradbury, at a conference some months later, and I shared comments about our production. He took selected material I proffered, examined a few pages, and said, "I think I would have liked my words read in this way."

Another representative of the science fantasy realm saw his writing come to life in stories I adapted from his fertile mind—that of Arthur Clarke. Unusual futuristic attire on the readers, and a block-filled set which extended into the auditorium of an old theatre helped bring a distinct vision to the stories. The audience was seated on risers which had the listeners actually on the old stage, looking down on the readers. All of the unusul elements joined in the production I called "And the Universe Ceased to Exist."

One year, I ventured into the elegantly strange, if not outright weird, mind of Stephen King. "Oohs, ahhs, and ughs" were shared reactions to adaptations of stories such as "The Lawnmower Man," and "The Silver Bullet." The set, created in an ONU ballroom accented the tenor of the stories. It had far more suggestive qualities than most Readers Theatre productions. Slatted wood sections, odd step units, high platforms, all with light shining from beneath, enhanced the strange, mysterious, eerie "Tales of Terror and Imagination."

Other productions brought to many non-theatre majors opportunities to share literature in numerous forms. Two short stories, "Why I Live at the P.O.," and "Lily Daw and the Three Ladies," introduced the work of Eudora Welty to the new readers and their audiences. This program, also staged in the intimacy of the octagonal Elzay Art Gallery, had the readers on swivel stools seated on white rectangular blocks of varied heights. In soft, black caftans and white turbans, the women readers created an evening of high humor in what we affectionately called "A Touch of Laughter."

"Voices of Women," a compilation of prose, poetry, and dramatic pieces by and about women, had ten young students to whom I had taught oral interpretation. The women almost jumped at the chance to participate in what became an annual event. These readers headed campus organizations, held offices in political arenas, and, by far, represented the best leaders in the student community of the university. The messages they shared during a Women's Week Celebration touched the minds and hearts of both women and men in the audiences. Readers and listeners alike found the power of their own "voices" from that production.

For "Tell Me How the Story Ends," I again compiled a variety of literary pieces. However, on the occasion of the Faculty Seminar, all the literature— humorous and serious—focused on communication—or lack thereof— in our social contacts. Again, the octagonal Elzay Art Gallery provided a fascinating venue for professors and staff who were new audiences to Readers Theatre. For example, the evening, visited with the likes of Charlie Brown, Lucy, and Linus, brought both laughter and sensitivity. In addition, George and Martha brought out the vicious communication battle in "Who's Afraid of Virginia Woolf." In all the literature, the hope for improved, and, indeed, beautiful communication was sought. The request for repeated performances seemed to indicate the success of our endeavors, and the need for civility of discourse.

The quirky, close to hysterical, humor created by Peter Cooke, Alan Bennett, and Dudley Moore brought open laughter and applause prior to, during, and following the presentation of "Good Evening." The material which I adapted was originally presented as revue sketches in London. To add another element of grace and humor to the introductory material, I had the all-male cast, dressed in white-tie and-tails, circulate among entering and seated audience members to whom they offered chocolate-covered-cherries, and a cheery, "Good Evening. So nice of you to come." Thus, the "proper" tone was set for the various sketches. My favorite to have directed involved "Matthew"— of Mark, Luke, and John fame—serving as a reporter, complete with a Press Card in the band of his fedora, still attired in tie and tails. With a colored robe over his shoulders, and carrying a shepherd's crook, Arthur L. Shepherd, out tending his imaginary flock of sheep, recognized "Matthew" from the current issue of "The Bethlehem Star." The interview centered on the birth of the Christ-child, the three kings as "poofs," and a distraught Joseph who was tired of the whole affair with the angel. When Matthew inquired about the atmosphere in the stable, Arthur simply observed, "Smelly. Yes, it was smelly. The animals had no sense of occasion whatsoever." The fine work by the gentlemen-readers brought only extensive amounts of chuckling, laughing, and delightful applause. For me, that Readers Theatre production provided the best of a "Good Evening."

The above recitation of some representative productions, for which I created and directed the material, brings a smile of remembrance of all the work, and, especially, the shared mutual regard for readers, audiences, and me.

That does bring us full circle, back to "The Earth Rocked Me"—my last Readers Theatre production. All aspects of the production—all the individuals involved—were touched by Sandburg's thoughts. The hours of rehearsal, the hours of technical crew construction, the hours of planning by the front and back-of-house staff were immeasurable. But, those hours were accomplished with pleasure. As creator-director, I was affected from moment-to-moment, not only during the run of the show, but also during those times I sat alone reading and arranging Sandburg's words to give voice to his ever-so-human thoughts.

"The beginning is being born...." I chose that line to open the show, to set the tone, the vision for the audience. I selected poem after poem, prose piece after prose piece, and songs to build the life of the people. I read and re-read the choices silently, and then aloud. The latter was vital to the process; because, in reading aloud, Sandburg's thoughts would be re-created in the minds of the audience members. They would see his visions, they would grasp his laughter, they would wince at his poignant observations. They would be in the hands and hearts of each cast member.

The Stambaugh Studio Theatre embraced Sandburg's world. The audience resided on three sides of a figurative earth. The round set was our earth, blue-fabric covered, with irregular-sized units on which the readers sat, walked, stood. Many colors from lighting instruments filled the set and its "owners" of that special earth. Our earth was set at a slant, raked low at first-row audience height, rising upward to eight-feet-high at its imaginary "pole." The earth was its own exciting entity. The house lights dimmed to black, then slowly a rich blue color on the set evolved to a pale blue as the readers entered the scene and crossed to their first positions on the "earth." Five young women, five young men inhabited this earth. Their costumes were comprised of khaki slacks, brightly-colored turtlenecks, and black notebooks—each with a complete script inside. Each reader knew the words and lines perfectly. Those notebooks indicated re-creation of the literature for each audience member. As the light on the readers and earth changed, notebooks were opened simultaneously, and those first words "began."

For ninety minutes, the audience was captured by their earth. The cast shared Sandburg's words which told a story of mankind. The readers and the audience members saw the beauty of the words, heard the sounds of the words, tasted the texture of the words. They absorbed the sadness and the joy of the people of their earth. Tears came to audience members' eyes, and flowed freely as they grasped touching meanings in the stories, as they laughed with abandon at jokes and proverbs. All the while, they held close to their hearts and minds the re-created works.

I felt a thrill as I watched the magic that is theatre occur. I closed my eyes and listened to the chosen words: "The earth rocked me in a cradle of winds...." "Behold the proverbs of a people." "... and the wind holds that barn up on the other side." "... What a hell of a way to run a railroad." I, too, knew every word and action, and I, too, participated in the magic of each performance.

"The Earth Rocked Me" was the last Readers Theatre production I created. Its success for all participants was part of my own success. Yet anxiety plagued me, and it was not the usual kind of concern over all aspects of a presentation. I felt a fear that the production was not to be "good enough." By that, I mean I feared negative assessment of my development of the script, the casting of the students, of the mounting of the production, of me. That deep-seated anxiety tormented me every hour. It was an assault on my senses. It began when I agreed to create a show. It did not end on the final night when the last audience member left the theatre. The doubt was, and still is, there like an anvil I think I will drag forever. I wondered, and wonder still, if it is possible that the chain to that anxiety would ever corrode and break.

In the end, I hope sometime I may find nurturance when I recall "The Earth Rocked Me." Somehow I feel I may remember most strongly and lovingly the final moments of the production. I will see the "earth" go dark. I will see the one reader step from the "earth" into a solo white beam of light. I will hear her say:

"I am more than a traveler..."

Fade to deep blue. Fade to black.... Fade to hope.

THANK YOU TO A FRIEND

What does one say about a companion of nineteen years? Many things. I was not her mother. She was not my baby. She allowed me to be her friend. Perhaps, I was a bit awed by her lineage from the Egyptian goddess Bastet. I don't think she was awed by me. However, with her I could be at peace, and I could learn to understand my world. And, I could see.

Letters to Pipkin

This work is about her—she would approve of that. The letters to her tell about her singular character—she would approve of that. The days of each letter convey only unconditional love—she would approve of that.

She was a cat. This furry-feline, pewter-gray, silver-pawed, golden-eyed, being leaped into my life September 15th, 1995. This strikingly beautiful being departed from my life December 13th, 2013.

We became and remained unwavering friends throughout every day, week, month, and year. We spoke each morning: I with a gentle "Good morning, Pip." She with a soft, lyrical "uh-mm." For breakfast, I often wanted a hot mug of Folger's Simply Smooth coffee and a bowl of Special K cereal. She wanted Fancy Feast Mornings with wild trout, eggs, and veggies in a cream sauce. Hm-mm...

In the first days of our relationship, I explored possible monikers for the seven-month-old kitten. I was always enchanted by Ray Bradbury's "The Halloween Tree." In that story, an ancient fellow drew all the children to find the little one whose love had embraced them all. And, they did find that love in their dear friend called Pipkin, just as I did in one small cat I named Pipkin. During our early years together in Ohio, she played, ate, and slept—lots. I worked—lots, and too often left for the university at 8:00 a.m. and returned at 8 or 9 or 10:00 p.m. I would find her stretched out on the sofa. She would yawn and look at me, as only a cat can, to express, "Oh… it's just you again." When we migrated to Colorado, Pipkin played, ate, and slept—lots—on my lap or with a paw securely attached to my thigh as I reclined on the sofa. Since I was retired, I was home almost all day. However, when I did leave, if only for a few minutes, and return, Pipkin would meet me at the edge of the entry-hall tile, and let me know in no uncertain terms, with a critical yowling meow, that she had been neglected and abused.

However, she was always present to give comfort during months when I could not see while my eyes were healing from cornea surgeries. As my health improved, Pipkin's health began to decline. In early summer of 2013, her illnesses gradually became worse, yet her spirit did not weaken. The snuggling became ever more important when we went three-times-per-week for what I called her "go juice." We became a fixture in the lives of the doctors and staff at the Front Range Veterinary Clinic. When I had phoned, I had always said, "This is Pipkin's friend calling. She needs some K-D kibbles." or "She needs a check-up." or "She wants…." And those people always knew her, as she aged to become a gracious, elderly lady.

But, then, that day came when I last said, "This is Pipkin's friend…." After nineteen years together, she and I parted—each remembering and knowing we will always and forever be friends. And so, I offer selections from the letters I have written to Pipkin. A dear person told me that she wrote of special times she had with her dog that had passed away. That act helped her remember Parker in happier days, and eased the burden of loss. Pipkin and I, through the letters, still speak in our special way.

Fri.-20 December 2013 (7:08 a.m.)

Pipkin, I looked for your furry warmth when I woke up. It seems odd not to see you curled up on the bed. I felt I had to get moving to get ready to provide some breakfast for you—fresh K-D kibbles, fresh Ocean Whitefish and Shrimp classic soft food, fresh Turkey and Giblets with gravy. That preparation was followed by a bit of ice water in your large glass mug. I loved your enthusiasm when your appetite was at its best.... I'm so sad you felt obligated to eat when I placed your food right at your mouth. I thought you couldn't smell the food when you'd walk away. But, then you'd come back to nibble a bit on your own time. Smart Pip.... Pipkin, it's been just a week since I was last with you—holding you close as all was prepared to help you leave that tired ill body, and find a new freedom. Your beautiful loving essence knows all now—all about living in a universe of no pain, no illness, a universe where care and love are unconditional for all. You have your place as a "god"—as the ancients regarded you.... Well, my little "god," I miss you—miss you in all your loving ways.... Pip, I have to not write for a bit now.

Sat.-21 December 2013 (2:51 p.m.)

Dear Pip... I'm a "little off-base" at the moment. I want to write to you and about you. Of course, what I say you already know. But, maybe you'll enjoy my recalling events and thoughts… I say I'm a bit "off-base" because I am tired and want to nap. But, there are many tasks to do. Yet, I really want to sit with you for a long time…. Hey, little one, remember— but, of course, you do—coming to sit at the front edge of the ottoman with only a bit of your black nose, your gold eyes, and gray tips of your ears showing. You watched me, as I read, wrote, talked on the phone or chatted with visiting friends, never making eye contact with you. You just waited and waited. Then, if I just "happened" to catch your eye, you immediately—so lightning fast—jumped onto the ottoman and then to my lap for "snuggling purposes!"… I wish you could now.

Sun.-22 December 2013 (8:25 a.m.)

Well, Pip, the coming days will be getting longer by seconds and minutes. The sun's arc will begin to change and there will be more sunlight in places on the stairs to the loft and on the living-room floor. I loved watching you move from sun-spot to sun-spot. Often your fur was hot to touch. I wonder how you could absorb so much heat…. But, near the end of our time together, you slept on the heat register in the floor in the loft. It seemed that for a few hours which became days and nights you stayed there almost prone across the register's surface. Were you getting cold inside? I think your illnesses might have caused that chill. I think you were also isolating yourself during those days. That last night when you left our bed, and I found you in the loft made me fear for you—or maybe the fear was for myself. I feared the loss for me…. And, I feel that night again. Tears come, little one. I want you with me. But, I want you to feel free from my needs.

Thur.-26 December 2013 (11:45 p.m.)

Dear Pip... I want to see you coming around the corner from the kitchen, eyeballing my ice-water in the glass mug, getting up on the ottoman, stretching to the side table, reaching to the glass, pawing gently toward it. "It's mine." said by me did no good. You had a sense of purpose. You wanted "that" glass. So, to satisfy you, to meet your demand, I would grasp that heavy glass, filled with ice cubes and water, and place it on the floor. Oh, how you jumped down to it so fast, and began seriously (while inwardly laughing at me?) lapping the icy water. How many years did you do that? I wish you were here tonight so that we could go through what became a ritual, my dear little gray one.

Fri.-27 December 2013 (7:15 p.m.)

Hi Pip... In a while, our friend Mo is coming to watch a bit of TV, and open some holiday gifts.... You would enjoy, not only playing in all the tissue paper, but also playing in my lap and chatting. Hey, do you remember "our chats?" We really talked to each other—I in English, you in Cat-lish. That word I coined sounds awful, doesn't it? But, little one, my skill with your language was far more limited than your skill for mine. I think you cleverly enjoyed my difficulties.

Sun.-29 December 2013 (11:30 p.m.)

Dear Pipkin... Cried for you today as I wrote two holiday cards. It didn't seem much like a holiday, though. I miss you—missed you terribly as I wrote to Jean. She had three kitties once. She, too, knows of loss.... I want you to know, my dear friend, that some people are suggesting that I get a kitty to care for as I did for you—that there is a kitty that needs me.... But, I want you to know that I can think of you, only you—now. I "see" you, Pipkin, coming down the stairs from the loft. In your wonderfully efficient way, you almost bounce on your back legs. I "see" you waiting to look out the front door when I come in.... Well, I'll think on those things as I go to bed wishing I could "see" you next to me.

Wed.-1 January 2014 (10:45 p.m.) —New Year's Day

Hello, Pip.... Today was supposed to be a special day, an introduction to a new year with fresh ideas and possibilities for living well—especially a day for loving, loving kitties....... If you were here in your beautiful, soft, furry body, I would allow you to snuggle on my lap, to creep up to rest on my chest, to chat with me as I chat and ask you questions about which you would answer yes/no/perhaps/not sure.... How did you know how much you helped and calmed me when inside I was confused, anxious, or angry?... When that wonderful, intuitive person, Kathryn, told me that she connected with your essence, your spirit, you were not in "your body" as I knew it. You left the illness of it here. She saw your essence caring for a little bunny. She saw "green," but it didn't seem like grass. It was soft, almost something one could sink into. The green was emerald in color—a color which is wonderful and powerful. It is a healing color. And, Kathryn observed that you may be a healing kitty—a "healing essence." She thought you may have been that way here on this earth. I recall many incidences of life you gave to me. Was coming to the sofa from the warmth and protection of our favorite leather chair a "healing" as you attached yourself to my left thigh, and reached out to place a paw, your right paw on my jeans? I think "yes" is what you'd say so modestly and shyly, though with a purpose…. Kathryn also sensed you were at peace, were happy to be—to be doing what you've always desired. She said many caring, many loving things about you. And, I felt there were more that had no words. I am so happy for you. I am so thankful the many years we spent together gave me peace. Near the end of your earthly life, I was so angry at little things that would occur. I cursed. I expressed hate of myself in horrible ugly words. But, I did want to be sure you didn't think that I was directing my remarks at you. You continued to love—you didn't avoid me when those awful times occurred.…Thank you—always with love—love of your essence, your being.

Mon.-6 January 2014 (3:00 p.m.)

Pip, my dear kitty. Some thoughts today: I always felt you knew so much—about our relationship—about people in general. Your perception skills were sharp…. I feel guilty about the times I lost my temper in dealing even with little issues. I lost my temper a lot in the past year. There was lots of anger that grew exponentlally. I've not expressed anger so much in the past weeks—at things outside me. I wonder if the outer anger came from frustration—inner unspoken fear that at some point in time I would not have you here. Pip, I know you're in a peaceful, better place, spirit healed, nurturing essence active. But, I miss so many things, such as your playing with that scraggly catnip mouse. I had put it away when… Hm-m. I feel tempted to go to the garage to get it—to keep it near me, as you kept it near you. Pip, I must let my thoughts of you go for now. We'll chat later, my friend.

Thur.-9 January 2014 (10:30 p.m.)

Hello, my dear friend…. Today was strange. I woke up at 10:30. Imagine that. You'd have had me awake to feed you many hours before…. I wanted you today. I felt guilty. I felt I had not done enough for you. Pip, I'm sorry. I'm so very sorry. Sorry for losing our reality here. Sorry that I cannot be with you in your place now. Just sorry. Today I saw months, then weeks, then days and hours go by—until 12:30, December 13th, 2013. You were so calm when I placed you in your carrier. Then there was the Clinic—the room with Dr. Brett, Jill, Peg—the warm blanket—the placement of the IV port. I stroked your soft furry head. You departed from us so quickly…. I hope you were not afraid as you travelled to a peace—to a peace without a sick little body—to a peace with the essence of you. Pip, I want to be with you, but I don't know how—how to cross a barrier to your place, to your peace…. Pip, did you grasp what happened? Do you grasp what happens now? I watched so often as you followed the sunlight across the living-room, curling up to sleep in the rays. Did you follow the sun on that December day? Something was there for you to follow—and, I could not follow you. I say it every day, so many times a day—I want to be with you. So, in my own way, I will be with you, my little friend…. I promise I will be with you—always.

Wed.-15 January 2014 (8:22 a.m.)

Hi there, beautiful lady… Oh, to feel your soft fur, to rub the stop of your nose today. I feel rushed, but want to spend some time with you. Am having the breakfast you would know: vanilla yogurt, raisin oatmeal, and, of course, my coffee with chemical cream. Your fondness turned toward the taste of: trout, green veggies, and egg, until your appetite wandered to the simple creamy salmon.... Hm-m, I wonder if your change in taste meant the inflammatory bowel disease had caused more swelling and pain.... I guess there was a terrible inevitability that the disease would turn cancerous. Pip, I'm so sorry that all happened. I would have taken that on myself—if I could.... You know, little one, even as ill as you were, you cared for me. I think of that when you came to bed and snuggled under the covers. I think of that when you insisted on getting up on my legs, lap, and chest to chat. I think of that when you glued your little body to my thigh as we sat on the sofa. You did those things for your comfort—and for mine. You gave of yourself to me. You nurtured. Now in your special, wonderful place you may nurture others, other animals or maybe humans. I'll think on that today.

Sun.-19 January 2014 (3:30 p.m.)

Hello, Pip... Are you enjoying warmth today? I don't know if you sit in the rays of the sun bathed with all you desire? As an essence, is this possible? I can imagine you extending your warmth in a nurturing way to other essences. I recall so vividly how we both felt the sun's rays come through the high south windows and gradually move around to shine from the west windows. You were quite skilled in keeping in the center of the warmth. Yes... you have the award for holding and sharing the warmth. Today, the sun reminds me of you. It reminds me of healing. It reminds me of the goodness you gave. You allowed me to see unconditional love. I thank you for that gift.

Sun.-16 February 2014 (6:20 a.m.)

Hi, Pipkin… and how are you today? I couldn't write to you on the 13th. There was too much sad remembrance that day. But, now it's the 16th…. Our two special friends were here last evening for the customary crackers, cheeses, celery, and apple-slices knoshing. You liked to lick salt from my crackers when we snacked, but were never into cheese eating. Remember how you stretched over to my plate from the ottoman, thinking "Eureka, I have found it!" That was followed by your version of "No way!"… Movies were on the agenda last night. You would have liked "My House in Umbria"— prime time for snuggling. Pip, I write to tell you these things, but I know you already "know" all these things from where your being is. I feel you still attempt to nurture me. You keep me going—keep me living now as you did when you were here.

Mon.-17 February 2014 (12:23 p.m.)

Pip—I need to write here. You know all I am to write, don't you?… I talked to Kathryn this afternoon. How wonderful it was to make contact with her again. Such a lovely lady! Her laugh, as you may know, is thoroughly delightful and contagious. And, Pip, she loves you. Meeting with you was a warm event for her. You allowed her to sense your spirit-essence, and you told her the most touchingly beautiful sentiments about life. I love you for allowing Kathryn into your world—for allowing her to share that with me….

She will try to reach out to you tomorrow. She knows many days and weeks have gone by, and you may have changed—moved on into other places or roles. I feel you still are nurturing to those beings around you—just as you were to me. Kathryn reminded me of the emerald green she felt when she saw your spirit-essence. I told her of my affinity for emerald green in grasses, in the lining of a protective robe that figures importantly in the story I wrote called "My Child, My Little One." And you, my dear little friend, may also be loved and be protected by that "green."... So, do share feelings with that unique lady, do continue your loving, nurturing ways. All I say is with love and gratitude today, Pip.

Wed.-5 March 2014 (10:10 p.m.)

Hi there, my friend... It's been several days since I last wrote to you—not because I don't think of you. I do—many times each day. Today I don't feel well. My hips and my thighs ache so deep into the muscles and nerves. This makes sitting possible for only a few minutes. I remember recent occasions when you hid your illness, and I unceremoniously put you off my lap so I could quickly stand and walk to relieve my pain. What an obliging kitty you were.... I have some soft, ocean-wave music playing now. It's quite comforting, isn't it. I sit here in our leather chair warming my hands with our unique coffee mug on which I write your name.... You know all this, but I have a need to tell you. If you were on my lap, my legs and thighs wouldn't ache so much right now. I suppose I could go to the loft to get the soft throw on which you often slept. That tan, sheepskin-like throw could warm me just as you did.... I wish I knew what you were doing now. Maybe listening to my thoughts? Oh, Pip, the tears of memory come tonight. My mind sees you, not only in the last minutes we shared—but also in the last warm snuggling days before we parted to our separate existences. There will always be tears of love for you, Pipkin.

Sat.-22 March 2014 (1:21 a.m.)

Good Evening, little lady. Perhaps I should be saying Good Morning given the late hour. Hm-m.... Remember how disgusted and frustrated you'd get when I was awake this late into the night? You would be sleeping in our chair. Then, at one point in time—11:30, or 12:30—you'd come over by the chair at the dining table where I was working, and stalk me, meow a bit, circle around the chair, meow a bit again for a treat that signaled we must go to bed.... So, I'd give in, knowing you were, indeed, right about time needed for sleep. I'd go to the bedroom to turn down the covers, trying to beat you before you got up on the bed to sneak under the comforter. In the winter, you'd squirm under the down comforter. In the summer, though, you'd lie on the cool sheets by my pillow. In all seasons, I'd stroke you between your ears, between your shoulders blades, and down your sides. You'd turn so that I could gently pet the soft delicate fur on your tummy.... Well, it's off to bed for now. Know that I'll think of you as I drift off to sleep.... Love to you, ever the warm one.

Fri.-28 March 2014 (7:15 a.m.)

Good Morning, Pipkin.... How has the week gone for you? I think of you each day as I catch "glimpses" of you carefully negotiating your way up the stairs to the loft in the evening, and then almost bounding down to be sure to catch your breakfast in the morning light.... I still wonder about the concept of day and night in your "place." I guess that's what we earthbound-beings take for granted. Right now, the sunlight of the morning is touching the tips of the deep, blue-green-colored spruce and the long-needled pine trees we observed every day. Do you have a sense of curling up and sleeping as you did in your favorite nooks in the living-room? We all have a need to sleep in our lives. Hm-m, maybe that too is an earthbound concept.... But, Pip, I have a feeling you "see" all the essences of sunrises and sunsets. Remember, the photos I took of our visions of sunrises and sunsets from Maine and Florida. They were beautiful. But, that striking gold sunset photo of clouds above the mountains from our balcony rivals any taken on the trips to Sheepscott Bay and to Melbourne Beach. Ah, Pip, we both loved the sun. To touch your fur was wonderfully comforting. I'm thinking about you and that comfort, as I do every day. And, I'm thinking of my earthbound-self, and wishing it were with you.

Mon.-31 March 2014 (9:00 p.m.)

Good Evening, my dear Pipkin.... I thought I'd write to you tonight, and this is a good time. I feel sort of numb, Pip.... Oh, I went to the salon to have my hair cut and styled today. What's a person to do with my gray hair, Pipkin? You, in your gracious years, did not have to worry about getting gray hair. All your fur was already gray, but it was a beautiful pewter-gray with occasional little flecks of tan. Your delicate paws were a beautiful shade of gray flowing into silver. And, you were ever so impeccable in caring for yourself. Even as your illness progressed, your appearance was striking.... Pip, what could I have done to help you, what could I have done?... Beyond your beauty on the outside was your beauty on the inside. And that's not a trite statement about you. You loved the sun, the warm air, also solitude. You did allow me to be your companion. So often, as you situated yourself on my lap, you would climb up onto my chest, then almost to my neck and left shoulder. You'd place your head on my shoulder and carefully view the surroundings—the mission-style Tiffany-like lamp, the oak nesting-table, and, of course, our frequent guest. You watched Mo ever so closely, and then you slipped down to walk the edge of the sofa to look more carefully at her. You chose just to look, not to snuggle with our guest. I thought that was wise. You assuaged my potential jealousy by not snuggling with her. Selfish wasn't I?…. Last night I wanted to have you by me, Pipkin. I had a bit of a meltdown as I "talked" to you before I gave in to sleep. I've said it so many times since I last held you on that December day. I didn't want you to go—to leave me…. "To sleep, to be no more, my little one."… I still want you here with me, or for me to be with you. But, as I've also said before, or asked: What is "there?" Is it a place? What is "place" in your present essence? I do want to know. A thought: If I sought now to join you with the act I keep always as an option, would I then be with you? The fear that I might not holds back the option. I'm so sorry, Pipkin. Sometimes I don't know what I want…. My dear little one, I must stop here. I must end these thoughts…. I feel the dampness of tears. They are for us. Tears and their accompanying saltiness help hold memories…. Pipkin, remember and let your being be with me in all my weakness. Let me be like you, my wonderful lady.

⌒

Letters to Pipkin concludes here with the entry on March 31st, 2014. Many additional letters carry forward the relationship between Pipkin and me. Thoughts and events similar to those from December through March emerge in letters written during weeks that follow. In them, I continue to remark about Pipkin's earthly-life. I continue to ask her about her essence—her being—the where, the what, the how. Not knowing any precise answers frustrates me still. That feeling, no doubt, will persist as I write, as I think about her. Pip gave so much to me—and still gives so much to me—she would approve of my saying that. Pip offered—and still offers unconditional love to me—she would approve of my saying that. That golden-eyed-feline allowed me to see into her heart. She comforted me when my sight—literally and figuratively—was in jeopardy. She comforted me when doubts and fears about my own when, what, and how inserted themselves into my life. She comforted me when.... That curious young kitty—that gracious elderly cat—that was Pipkin. The remarkable essence—the nurturing being—that is Pipkin.... She was— and is—and will be—always my friend.

THE BOOK
OF CECILIA

Fifty-five years ago, I met a young woman, Cecilia or Cec, who became and has remained a treasured friend. During the time we shared as boarding-school students at St. Scholastica Academy, she sensed when I was almost overwhelmed with anxiety and depression. And, she drew out my feelings and got me to share them with her. Even today she listens with concern, and listens with care. Then, she offers gifts to help me during dark times. The gift of humor. The gift of laughter. The gift of a perspective on life that always brings a smile. She sees her glass as half-full, and wonders if I see mine as half-empty. I respond that I don't even have a glass. Enter more laughter. And, enter stories of her singular adventures. Those enterprises, those "things about Cec" do provide for me a clear, beautiful vision of life. Because of Cec, I want to see.

The Thing About Cec

"Sir,... sir! I cannot understand you. Speak up, sir. What is your problem? Sir, please carefully state your name and address and the purpose of your call. Sir?" The 911-caller refused to clarify the emergency situation. Precious minutes passed with more questions, and the desperate-sounding breathing of the caller continued. At some point, the Dispatcher for the police department, the sheriff's department, and the state patrol at Glenwood Springs, Colorado, began to think the problem was actually an obscene caller—a "breather." "Would you get off the line now," and other angrier requests and orders were made, but the caller remained on the phone and ignored the admonitions. The disgusted Dispatcher filed a nuisance suit, and the head office in Denver finally notified her regarding the address of the nefarious 911-caller. It was determined that the call was being made from a phone programmed for a 911-emergency. By simply pressing any button, the call would be made. The police were sent to the home, managed to enter, and picked up the abusive caller. And, who was the abusive caller? "He" was a dog, a small, innocent, German Shepherd puppy, that had jumped onto a table, hit the phone, and then breathed excitedly each time he heard the Dispatcher's voice. The attending officers then got on the phone to contact the frazzled Dispatcher. "Hey, gal, we've got a four-legged perp. here. What was that emergency again? Please clarify. Do you think it was an empty puppy-chow bowl?... Better send the EMT-squad ASAP! He's still a lickin', and slobberin', and breathin' kind of heavy. Over and out."

This particular Dispatcher also had concerns with other callers. One particularly persistent woman phoned the office to inquire in an irritating nasal tone, "What's the weather like today?" Morning after morning, day after day, week after week, the same whining call came in. The Dispatcher, who sat in an enclosed, secure, interior office would dutifully provide the woman with current weather conditions. Finally, the Dispatcher had enough. The usually reserved, collected person calmly picked up the handset. "Excuse me, ma'am. If you want to know what the weather is, just open your damn window and stick your head out!" The calls for the daily weather conditions ceased. Charges for such untoward behavior could have been levied against the Dispatcher. However, her directive to the woman received cheers as the "order" circulated among the ranks of the police, sheriff, and state patrol. It was too choice, too delightful, too exceptional to deserve any disciplinary action. After that incident, however, numerous questions began to come in to the Dispatcher: "Hey, gal, is it raining heavy enough for me to wear my official police rain- gear?" or "Excuse me, ma'am, is it cold enough for me to wear my pink, fuzzy, long-johns today?"

One may feel prompted to ask, "Who was that Dispatcher?" And, all the law enforcement personnel would most respectfully state: "Cecilia McNulty Woods."

The "thing" about Cecilia—Cec as she was called—is that, prior to her career and work and frequent quirky ways with those special law enforcement folk, there were indications that not all was "usual and customary" in her life. I came to learn of this delightful individual's adventures when we were boarding-school roommates.

Cecilia McNulty entered St. Scholastica Academy in Canon City, Colorado, in September of 1958. "Cec" didn't really want to enroll in an all-girls' school, even one that had a fine history since its founding in the late 1800's. What Cec wanted was to be home in Glenwood Springs, Colorado. So, with her Lifetime Railroad Pass in hand, Cec attempted to sneak away from the Academy and ride the Denver and Rio Grande train to her hometown. Each time during her freshman year when Cec headed down Pike Street to the station, two nuns from the school would appear to stop her in transit and return her to the Academy.

Only later did Cec learn that two elderly ladies carefully watched her progress from their rocking-chairs in the comfort of the front-window of their optimally-situated Victorian home. The duo always phoned the Academy principal to report Cec's progress. The Sisters of the Order of St. Benedict understood Cec's desire to leave, but saw the situation just a bit differently. The Academy was not a prison from which to escape. Thus, "Cecilia, dear" never accomplished the "thing" to catch that train—ever.

"Miss Manners" admonitions to sit, stand, and walk properly as befitted a young lady in her freshman year at the Academy were the sort of "things" lost on Cec. In her estimation, a "lady" did not need a book on the top of her head to be successful. She also considered coursework about the "proper way" to walk—to carry oneself with grace— next to impossible when thirty-to-forty young ladies in uniforms of navy-blue, A-line skirts and blazers trouped, in no particular order, to Canon City's Main Street. Excitement grew among the girls who were permitted to leave campus every Wednesday precisely at 3:30 p.m. "Town-pers"—permission slips to skip part of study hall and shop downtown—were granted to those who had dutifully submitted their course homework.

Cec considered walking on past Main Street and slipping away to the train station. However, the freedom with friends distracted Cec, and she focused on finding unusual foods not available in the school's Snack Bar. Items purchased might include soda-crackers, tuna-fish, smoked oysters, and like goodies. Foodstuffs such as these figured in late-night, after-lights-out, unapproved in-room picnics. Cec always handled the events with ease and minimal fear of demerits. It was just a "thing about Cec."

The topic of Cec and food revealed her desire for the finer tasteful features in a meal. She loved many different kinds of sweets. Chocolates. Strawberries. Ice Cream. And, without a doubt, Peeps. These were just a few that crossed her palate. In the spring, special breads captured her tastes. She nearly salivated at the thought of Irish Soda Bread and Hot-Cross Buns. Perhaps her heritage gave Cec a special proclivity for the former. The latter provided impetus for Cec to befriend the German Benedictine nuns who cooked all the food for the students and Sisters. Begging for Hot-Cross Buns became *pro forma* during Lent.

However, in other instances, Cec simply "five-fingered" the food she desired. Of course, breakfast for all the Academy residents was served after Mass each morning, and those services were led by an Abbey priest from the boys' school across town. Cec frequently had kitchen duties, which involved laying out Father Peter's breakfast in his special dining room. The "thing about Cec" during this task? She would pick out and eat one-to-two tasty bacon strips prepared by the kitchen nuns. At some point during this period in Cec's life, Father Peter discovered the young woman's thievery, but said nothing to chastise her. Rather, the kindly priest only asked the cooks to prepare more bacon for *him*, so that Cec could continue to have *her* two pieces of bacon each morning.

The religious influence of Catholicism pervaded so much of Cec's life at the Academy that her friends considered her quite devout and staunch in her beliefs. However, she was quite curious about those Protestants who inhabited several churches along the Pike Street route to downtown. Near the end of a town venture one Wednesday, Cec sneaked into the stately Methodist Church just in time for a funeral service—just in time to see a finely-suited dead man laid out in an open coffin. She—in her Academy attire—almost ran all the way back to the school. It was just one of those Cec "things."

A number of Catholic activities, inured in her system, did cause unusual difficulties for Cec and her cohorts. One Sunday afternoon, we SSA girls went downtown to attend a movie at McCormick's Theatre. Cec led the pack into the dim light of the first floor of the theatre. There she found an empty row of seats, made the Sign of the Cross, and kneeled— genuflected—as she always did in Chapel. This "Cec thing" created havoc. M.L., immediately behind Cec, bumped into her, and lost her contacts. As she knelt to find them, student after student piled on top of her and Cec, who was still kneeling religiously in the aisle. Laughter erupted from "townies" in the balcony from which all Academy ladies were barred because of the "the terrible things that went on up there." It was another Cec "thing" to always be intrigued by those "terrible things."

If one were to seek out other evidence of my roommate's devout nature, one need only check out her sacrifice during Lenten season our senior year. Cec chose to recite the complete: "Hail Mary, full of grace. The Lord is with thee. Blessed art thou among women, and blessed is the fruit of thy womb, Jesus. Holy Mary, Mother of God, pray for us sinners now and at the hour of our death." She chose to pray the lengthy exhortation each time she touched a doorknob. She did so. However, by the end of the second day of Lent, Cec realized she would never be on time to classes, to meals, to chapel, if she continued her "sacrifice." Thus, Cec chose to go to confession, to Father Peter. There she begged to be absolved of her good intention—her Cec "thing." The combination of entries and exits in all of the buildings comprising St. Scholastica Academy had just far too many doorknobs!

There also seemed to be a "thing about Cec" and the stunning, magnificent Colorado outdoors. Because she so appreciated such activities, Cec convinced classmate Margaret—Mac, as she was known—to help "ride herd" on some new freshman students. The two young women and four nuns accompanied the "newbies" on a trek to and around Red Canyon north of the city and campus. Crazy games, marginally skillful clambering over rocks, and mini-hikes provided a day of unabashed fun. When the time came to round up their charges to return safely to the Academy before dark, Cec and Mac were to find and bring along any freshman stragglers. The talkative duo chatted so much, and ambled so slowly, they became stragglers themselves. As dusk fell, they strolled quite near a decrepit 1800's cemetery. A "thing about Cec" was that she spooked easily. Suddenly, there was a movement of white passing slowly among the old limestone and marble headstones. Cec, startled by the ghostly apparition, began to run away and scream, "Ghost. Ghost. Dear Holy Mary, it's a Ghost!" At that point, the other-worldly whiteness moaned— actually a long low "mooo-o-o." Mac laughed hysterically and tried to catch Cec to calm her, to show her, and to explain that Cec's "ghost" was only a lonely, old white cow munching grass and wandering among the tombstones in the fading light.

Another of the many Cec "things" was her focused attention on the young gentlemen, the "heart-throbs" who resided at The Abbey, the boys' high school on the east side of Canon City. She wished she could play a trumpet, a clarinet, or a tenor saxophone, as I did. Then she would be able to go to band practice two times per week in the Abbey-Academy Band. There were at least six "heart-throbs" in that organization. And, Cec indubitably loved each of them.

Other Canon City "gentlemen" sparked Cec's interest. She and other SSA "ladies" sneakily removed screens from the corner windows of our rooms in Senior Hall. Those windows were closest to facing a nearby street. And, of course, they were far better for peering out at the town boys who circled the campus in their souped-up dragsters. Cec would situate herself so that the spotlights on the townies' car would shine on her. Years later, as they swapped stories of their young lives, Cec learned that one of those "Canon Boys," one in particular, had become her loving husband, Ralph Woods.

Of the many stories that have been circulated about Cec "things," one remained a secret among the women of Senior Hall, and undiscussed for nearly fifty years. Near the end of our senior days, Cec got involved in a little contest, a challenge as it were. The second floor Senior Hall was, indeed, a large wide hall bordered by the girls' two- three-or four-person rooms. The hall floor was highly polished wood, oak to be specific, made as slick as glass by the convent sisters who saw such cleaning a simple duty offered in prayer to God. The aforementioned contest involved all of us, black-and-white saddle shoes off, and white, cuffed, cotton socks on. An imaginary line crossed the width of the hall. The object of the game was to begin to run from one end of the hall as fast as possible. Upon reaching the line, the competing senior was to slide in her stocking feet as far as she could down the rest of the hall. The girl who slid the farthest beyond the "line" won the contest.

One evening, sans presence of the stern Senior Hall prefect Sister Agnes who was at chapel for prayers, we held our contest. All twenty-seven seniors— with Cec, of course—ran, slid, stopped, and measured their sliding distance. Challenges were made for a second run. Cec threw down the gauntlet. Runs began again. Cec took off like an Olympian in a 50-yard dash. She ran. She slid—and slid—right into the far wall of Senior Hall. But, the sound of the excited cheers could not drown out the sound of the shattering crash.

The force of Cec hitting the wall shook an old, wooden, square pedestal with an equally old, time-worn statue sitting on it. The statue swayed. The statue fell. St. Theresa of Avila lay in many large, many small shards on the highly-polished floor at the end of Senior Hall. There was an intake of all oxygen. Every senior came to peer at the remains. "What's going to happen? We're really sunk now!" "Be quiet. No we're not." whispered Cec. From her room, she quickly retrieved a bed sheet, and spread it on the floor. "Now, listen. Gather up every shard, no matter how tiny, and put it on the sheet." Cec herself carefully picked up the oddly undamaged head of the Saint, and with great respect, placed it on the sheet with the other fragments. "What do we do now?" Fear still pervaded the group. "Sh-sh. Wrap the sheet tightly around her—or what's left of her." "Then what?" "Be still.... Wait here. I'll be back in a moment."

In a couple of minutes, Cec returned with a large, worn, rough, gray, canvas laundry bag. She and Mac and M.L. thoughtfully, respectfully, sensitively "stuffed" the white sheet cum shards into the laundry bag. "OK, M.L., Mac, and I will dispose of the remains." "But, where can you do that? You can't put that in a dumpster." one anxious girl stated. "Be quiet as you can. Go back to your rooms. Act as if nothing has happened. The less you know the better." Fear. Dread. Then, calm. The Sisters were nowhere near. They were at Chapel for nightly prayers, so none would be aware of the fiasco.

The little company of three hefted the saintly bag and crept silently down the usually creaky stairs of the old Victorian dormitory. Fortunately, no alarm sounded when Cec unlocked and opened the rear door to the building. Wisely, Cec placed a rock to hold open the door slightly for their return. So, off they went, Cec leading Mac and M.L. to the north end of the campus near the apple and peach orchard. "Where are we going?" "Sh-sh. Just hang on to her." In quick order, they reached their destination—an old chicken coop. The obsolete structure had been on the property when the school was self-sustaining. It had been unused for decades, and, for some unknown reason, never torn down. Cec and company pried open the aged door, entered, and knelt carefully in the old, rotten straw and chicken droppings. With bare hands, the threesome dug a substantial hole. Into this rough-hewn grave, they gently placed St. Theresa—in her laundry bag shroud. They covered her, patted down the straw and chicken droppings, and recited the "Hail Mary" prayer. Mac and M.L. began to giggle. "Stop, you guys! We still have to get back into the dorm." So, the nefarious trio made it back without incident, supposedly without a single nun discovering the seniors' transgressions. The nun of Avila who had for so many years watched over Senior Hall, the nun of Avila whose pedestal now held an unassuming, old-fashioned, ceramic vase taken from a storage unit, became for Cec, for the seniors, for all time—Saint Theresa of the Chicken Coop.

It was just one of those "things about Cec.".…… Amen.

During my junior and senior years in high school—more specifically, in the boarding school of St. Scholastica Academy, I felt the distinct warmth and love of my roommates. I also had a delightful pleasure as I watched Cec and Mac, and others of us on occasion, participate in certain outrageous undertakungs. For me, the activites of the young women still provide inimitable glimpses of special times and lives.

The Bishop and the Nun

Standing in the side doorway to the school auditorium were a bishop—a prelate of the Diocese of Pueblo, Colorado, and a nun—a principal of St. Scholastica Academy in Canon City, Colorado. Bishop Charles Buswell, tall and imposing, exuded authority and discipline. Sister Mary Fabian, likewise tall and imposing, exuded authority and discipline. What they observed from their discreet post caused "What the hell is going on?" looks of astonishment. Of course, these two would never have verbalized "hell" or even have thought the word—maybe.

May I mention that earlier, the four-tiered, wooden, floor of the study-hall/auditorium was set with row upon row of folding chairs. That the stage with its sides and backdrop of royal blue, velvet drapes provided the scene for an additional twenty-eight folding chairs, placed at a slight angle in rows of seven. That a set of gray, metal risers stood at the base of the stage. That at the right side of the stage, situated on a twelve-inch high, six-foot-square dais, was an elegant, graceful, wooden, arm-chair cushioned in rich, red, brocade fabric, befitting its regal use-to-be. That around the large room and at either side of the stage, rested striking arrangements of white roses on dark walnut pedestals.

May I further mention that young women, students at St. Scholastica Academy—SSA as it was affectionately known—had worked to prepare the room, the chairs, the risers, the dais, and the flowers. The senior class president directed the activity to be accomplished as quickly and smoothly as possible. Once done with their respective jobs, the students left to ready themselves for the special occasion. However, one task remained. A stand with its attached microphone needed to be adjusted so that those persons— the invited guests—who would soon enter and be seated could easily hear the proceedings to come. And who was to adjust the stand and set the microphone level? Cec and Mac. Cecilia and Margaret, with pride in their electronic skills, positioned themselves at the mic and amplifier.

Now, their questionable electronic acumen was not what caused the dumbfounded reaction by the Bishop and the Principal. Mac, the amplifier adjuster, was wearing a white, percale sheet loosely wrapped around her, secured by a rosy-red, bungee-cord, belt. On her head was a like-colored hunting cap, with earflaps loosely tied up on top. Cec, the mic monitor, had secretly raided the Academy Chapel's vestry. She was attired with a white, lace surplice; a silver and gold stole around her shoulders; a white and gold miter on her head; and a gold crozier held securely in her left hand. Cec sat in the impressive chair on the dais, and made the Sign of the Cross as Mac knelt to kiss Cec's class ring and to receive her flimsy, diploma-like, piece of notebook paper from "Bishop Cec." Mac bowed and returned to her amplifier position as Bishop Cec rose to test the sound system and to give her address to the yet nonexistent audience.

"Oh, Blah, Blah, Blah... Academy history. Blah, Blah, Blah... fine Academy girls. Blah, Blah, Blah... your great future." On the "Blahs" went until—until Cec glanced at the auditorium doorway. Mac's eyes followed. They saw them—the two most authoritative people in their lives. The "Blahs" ceased. Panic ensued. Cec looked at Mac. Mac looked at Cec. Mac's bungee-cord slid to the floor along with her sheet. Cec could not remove quickly enough the miter which left her carefully coiffed hair flying in all directions, and the stole which became entangled in the surplice. The crozier she propped askew against the elegant chair. Cec and Mac froze for an agonizing moment. Then, as if the Holy Spirit came upon them, they disappeared—sort of like the Ascension. Actually, the two young ladies ran to ascend the flight of stairs to their senior hall rooms. They just knew the knife of Abraham was going to descend— with no pause this time.

However, no nuns came to judge and punish them. No one appeared to tell them they could not partake in the day's special activities. With fear in their eyes and lumps in their throats, Cec and Mac attired themselves in the real costume for the day. Along with their Academy cohorts, the young women put on new, stylish dresses, straight- seamed nylons, white—very white—gowns, and white—very white—mortar boards secured with a dozen bobby-pins, and white—very white—new shoes with slick soles (or was it s-o-u-l-s). With the senior hall prefect's meticulous guidance, all the girls lined up alphabetically. "Girls,... last name first, please," Sister Agnes noted.

Cec and Mac quivered visibly. Sister Agnes gave only a curious nod their way. The time for the event of the day had arrived. It was precisely 11:00 in the morning of June 1st, 1962. The event? Graduation Day for twenty-eight girls—now young women—from St. Scholastica Academy. The seniors were to continue a tradition that had begun in 1891—their commencement to a new life.

The graduates-to-be, now ready for one of the most important days in their lives, entered the auditorium. Mothers, fathers, grandparents, and relatives of all sorts stood in honor. Each girl, Cec and Mac included, somehow managed to execute the tricky, right foot, step-slide, left foot, step-slide to the sound of "Pomp and Circumstance," solemnly played by Sister Kathleen. Cec bit the inside of her cheek to restrain from giggling as she recalled the quirky nun's remark to her about "Pomp and Circumcision." With carefully balanced mortar boards, the seniors proceeded to their respective places on the stage. Sister Fabian followed, stood at the lectern, nodded for the women and the audience to be seated. Her welcoming words, warm and gracious, set the proper tone of respect for the occasion. She, then, stepped aside to permit Sister Agnes, also the choral leader, to direct the singers to their soprano and alto positions on the risers. It should be noted that Cec remained seated. She might "speak" well; but, singing was way beyond her pervue of expertise.

Appropriately, the choir opened with "The Star Spangled Banner." Another song, "America the Beautiful," followed. And, then, the women— they were young girls at that moment—sang a magnificent selection which they had all felt was "theirs." Sister Agnes had threatened dire consequences if any of them began to cry during the piece. However, when the words, "Oh, God of Spotless Holiness, Oh, God of Light and Splendor..." began, there were no dry eyes. Even Cec quietly sniffed in her place.

At last, following the ceremonial tradition of remarks by the Principal and by the Class President, His Excellency Bishop Buswell carefully negotiated the stairs to the stage. In all his finery, he moved to the microphone at the dais, and delivered a rather stuffy, stilted, obligatory address. In contrast to the speech, he turned with a certain theatrical flair, to sit in his special chair when he concluded the speech.

In her sonorous tone, Sister Fabian began the final portion of the ceremony. She read the name of each graduate. As her name was called, each senior rose, walked to the center of the stage, bowed to the assembled audience, turned to kneel at the feet of the bishop, and raised her left hand to grasp his left hand to kiss the finely cut, ruby-encrusted, gold ring of his office. Only then, did the bishop place the lambskin-covered diploma in the young woman's right hand. She rose, bowed to his Excellency, and bowed again to the polite applause of all the relatives.

When the "M" section of the alphabetical list of seniors was reached by Sister Fabian, Mac—the amplifier attendee previously noted—a.k.a., Miss MacLennon, rose. Her hands trembled. Her knees shook. But, Mac completed her journey to and from the bishop. Even though her face reflected a definite fear, to her credit she did not fall apart. Then, after a distinct pause, as if for special effect, Sister Fabian read the name of Cec—Cecilia Ann McNulty. Much trepidation had already situated itself in Cec's psyche. Now, came the test of her fortitude. She rose, and on wobbly, three-inch, heels, proceeded through the ritual and kneeled at the bishop's dais. She reached for his hand. He reached for her hand. He held it firmly as she kissed the brilliant ring. He did not release his grip, however. Slowly, he tipped his mitered head toward her and whispered, "My dear, you looked remarkable earlier today. And, my child, you gave a much better speech than I." With a slight smirk, a Sign of the Cross, and a word of congratulation, Bishop Buswell slipped Cec's white diploma into her hand. She rose, bowed to him, bowed to the audience, bowed to Sister Kathleen, bowed to Sister Agnes, bowed to Sister Fabian, bowed to her senior friends, and shakily made it to her seat. She was almost unaware of the rest of her fellow classmates, as they received their due honor.

Following the graduation ceremony, Cec and Mac, amidst all the happy confusion of families and friends, found each other. One look was all it took to break into silly grins and giggles. They gave each other a conspiratorial hug, and took a final journey to the last special event. Mac never again used her electronic skills. Cec's "Blah, blah, blahs" ended her SSA speaking career, except… except Cec desired to give one more speech—of apology—to the stern principal. She turned to do so for the nun at the High Benediction in the Academy Chapel. But, Sister Fabian quickly shushed Cec, and drew her close in an enveloping embrace of love.

The story of Cec and Mac, and the Bishop and the Nun probably could go on and on—at length. However, that tale would only be more "Blah, blah, and blahs."

Two small words that may denote visual acuity.
Two small words that may denote mental understanding.
Two small words for one small group of girls and for one not-so-small woman.
I See.

A Delectable Repast in One Act

The Entrees:

Tasty Tuna Fish. Select Smoked Oysters. Crisp Club Crackers. Premium Saltine Squares.

Firm Colby-Jack Cheese. Softened Crème de Brie.

The Scene:

St. Scholastica Academy, Canon City, Colorado. Specifically: a Senior Hall lined with rooms for the young women, and a single room for the prefect.

The Time:

1962. April. A Wednesday. Ten-o'clock p.m. Specifically: after evening study hall, after time to ready for bed, after the call for "Lights Out," after all the Sisters of the Order of St. Benedict had gathered in the school chapel for final prayers and Gregorian chants.

The Players:

"Cec" - the dynamic director of the activity. "V"- the scene technician. "ML" - the treat assembler. "R" - the crouch-in-the-corner-lookout-guard-because-they're- going-to-get-killed.

Four girls as adult as sixteen-year-olds can be. All anticipating a June-first graduation day. All having accrued various demerits for untoward behaviors during time as SSA boarding students. All having "served time" polishing floors, shining silverware, pulling dandelions, and dusting each library book. All being questionably bright and resourceful. All planning one last opportunity for an unapproved delectable meal with above stated items.

The Setting:

With the "lights out" directive in place and, of course, no light seeping in from behind the window coverings, coal-like blackness envelops the above cast of players in their Senior Hall room.

ML: "What do we do now?" [*said loudly*]

Cec: "Whisper."

R: "Grief. Here's my flashlight. Let's get some kind of light in here." [*said with force*]

Cec: "Whisper."

V: "I've got it. Here, drape this gauzy scarf over the dresser lamp." [*said with authority*]

Cec: "Whisper... Please."

ML: "OK, Cec. Just hurry up and get out our stash!"

R: "Our what?" [*said loudly with surprised fear*]

Cec: "Whisper... What don't you understand about the word whisper, guys?"

ML: "Hey, stash means food! Pul-lease. During town-pers today, Cec and I bought goodies at the Canon City Market."

V: "OK-OK... Get down on the floor, and spread everything out on my huge bath towel—the one covered with seashells."

R: "Oh, whoopee. Let's play: We're at the beach!"

Cec: "Hey, you two... a little cooperation here. ML, get those cans open. V, set down these paper plates and napkins from the Snack Bar. R, just sit near the door—as lookout."

R: "Lookout... Lookout? Excuse me, I'd like to eat, too."

Cec: "You will, ding-dong. You're sitting on the end of V's towel, aren't you?"

ML: "Listen up... here's the tuna fish and smoked oysters, I think. I can't see the little oysters. They seem dark and they look so tiny... Are you sure we're supposed to eat them?"

Cec: "For goodness sake, ML, just slap one on a cracker and take a bite."

V: "ML's right. They look weird. I'm sticking with the tuna fish and saltines."

R: "Don't be a chicken, V... Cluck, cluck, cluck." [*teasing loudly*]

Cec: "Hey, ladies! Whisper... I really mean it. We could get caught for sure." [*said with a bit of hoarseness*]

ML: "Given what we have, this layout actually looks good. I offer that we've done a superb job. Come on, try the Club Crackers with the Colby-Jack. I finally got it sliced. That Dining Hall knife you stole is dull—and I mean dull as a rock."

Cec: "Don't criticize our only utensil. I had a hard time sneaking that knife from Father Peter's breakfast tray. Those cooks kept eyeing my odd behavior."

R: "Not to worry, Cec. I say everything looks divine. Oh, pass the Crème de Brie, V—and a handful of the Club Crackers."

V: "So now you're going to give me orders? My orders for you are to hide your bunny-covered jammies. Rabbits better not go near this cheese."

ML: "Yea for V!" [*ML , V giggle uncontrollably*]

Cec: "Quiet down. My god, you'll wake the dead, you guys!"

V: "Oh, and Cec, you need to join R's PJs for the next Macy's Parade." [*ignoring Cec's directive*]

Cec: "And…just why would I team up with the likes of R?"

ML: "Cec, just look at your feet…"

Cec: "What are you jabbering about? Oh, I see, you're referring to my Great Aunt's Christmas gift. I'll have you know I'm very proud to sport these fuzzy, pink bunny slippers… Just look at the cute little nose and wiggley ears." [*feigning hurt feelings*]

[*The quartet of V, ML , Cec, and R continue to engage in "deep thought" chit-chat, regaling and topping one another with observations about a number of events involving the black-habited teachers.*]

Cec: "Listen up. I don't know a sharp from a flat. I don't dare try the Gregorian chants at Benediction. I just can't sing, but Sister Agnes keeps bugging me to participate in the graduation choir. It's pretty bad, guys."

ML: "You think that's bad. Just think of Sister Aurelia last term when she kept slowly backing away from Tinker- Bell in chemistry class."

V: "That's right! Tinker-Bell, was furiously pounding and grinding that mixture of chemicals with her mortar and pestle. She had the right combination to make gunpowder, but was totally clueless as to what she might blow up."

R: "Imagine Sister Audrey's huge gasp if her library books had been blown down Pike Street, clear to the middle of town."

Cec: "Poof... no more historical landmark."

ML: "Poof... No more golden stairs to the nun's common area."

V: "Poof... No more polishing wood bannisters until they glow like the sun."

R: "Well, personally I like the particular skills each nun possesses. Look at our SSA jax champion! Sister Fabian, our ever so principled principal, just gathers up her habit, kneels down on the floor, and plays it solo from two- sies through the entire set."

ML: "Right... I tried once—and only one humiliating once—to challenge her skills. I didn't have a chance after one-sies. She kept bouncing that red ball and grabbing up all the jax. You know, she was like a chess grandmaster—a holy terror."

V: "A holy terror... that's a good one!... Oh-a-a, guys... oops!" R: "What's with the oops?... uh-oh..."

Cec: "Friends, another holy terror may be coming down the hall."

ML: "What?... What's wrong, Cec?... Oh, my god!"

[At that point in the party, voices stop, chewing stops, fear descends as the quartet strains to hear.]

V: "Jesus, Mary, Joseph! It's coming… that walk… it's coming down the hall."

R: "I warned you guys… we are sunk."

V: "Yeah, sunk… we're drowning rats. We're getting caught in a rat trap!"

ML: "Holy Mary… I mean, oh god. I mean what do we do with the stash?"

R: "I warned you guys… we are sunk."

V, ML, Cec: "Yes, Miss R, we know you warned us. Now, shut up."

R: "OK—OK. But, V's rat trap door is going to open any minute. I warned you."

ML: "Quiet. Help me, dear God—and God forgive me… What the hell are we going to do with the stash?"

V: "Just shove it under the bed! At least we'll only get dragged in for not being asleep."

R: "Asleep? You've got to be kidding. We're up past hours. We've got a lamp on, covered with some ugly—sorry V—scarf. We're sitting in a circle on the floor like some ancient pow-wow. And, you think we'll get demerits for not being asleep. Where were you when God or St. Peter or whoever gave out common sense? And, by you, I mean all of you… including me!"

ML: "Give me your inhaler, V! I can't breathe… She's coming. I can hear her footsteps. Oh, God… no, not God, she's…"

V: "God, he's—no, I mean God, she's going to open the door… It's…"

[The doorknob is turned to open. The light switch is flipped to on. Extreme brightness fills the room. Then enters, in full Benedictine attire, a tall

woman, distinguished in accomplishments, stately in demeanor, one Sister Mary Agnes.]

Sr. Agnes: "I see... Girls?"

Cec, ML, V, R: "Good evening, Sister Agnes." [*sitting in frozen positions, in terror*]

[*Then, Cec calmly, and with purpose, extricates herself from the campftre-like circle, reaches for a plate of tuna ftsh, oysters and a few left-over Club Crackers, stands, semi-bows, and nods to Sister Agnes.*]

Sr. Agnes: "Ah-a... Girls?"

Cec: "We're having a few... uh, appetizers this evening, Sister Agnes. Which would you prefer on your crackers, tuna fish or smoked oysters?" [*said assertively*]

[*Pause... Very long pause.*]

Sr. Agnes: "Well... Cecilia. I believe I'll have the smoked oysters on the Club Crackers. Oh, may I sit here on this bed?" [*Pause... Moderately long pause.*]

ML: "Oh, yes, Sister Agnes. Oh, that will be fine, Sister Agnes. Oh, certainly that will be perfect, Sister Agnes."

[*Sr. Agnes sits, and looks down over her wire-rimmed glasses at ML , V, R, and Cec, who has resumed her place in the circle.*]

Sr. Agnes: "Girls…"

Cec, ML, V, R: "Yes, Sister Agnes. We're sorry. We can explain. We see…"

Sr. Agnes: "Sh-sh. Hush, you'll wake up all the other seniors, who, hm-m… are probably awake anyway."

Cec, ML, V, R: "Yes, Sister Agnes. Certainly, Sister Agnes."

Sr. Agnes: "Sh-sh, please…. What I want to say is that you rather not-so-bright young ladies actually seemed to believe that your secret meal was, indeed, secret."

Cec, ML. V, R: "Yes, Sister Agnes. We thought so. We…"

Sr. Agnes: "Shush, girls! Your, ah… secret was known all the way to the Chapel. Although it was difficult to distinguish the different smells of your various entrees, we sisters think the smoked oysters won the day— or night, so to speak…. [*smiles mischievously*] And, if you don't mind, girls, I'll have another Club Cracker with those delectably delicious smoked oysters."

Many nuns in religious Orders of the Catholic Church wore full habits
prior to certain freedoms for them granted by the Vatican II Council.
The habits, be they white as worn by the Dominican Order, brown by
the Franciscan Order, or black and white by the Benedictine Order, were
a distinctive mark of the professions of the women. Other Orders wore
similar combinations of styles and colors. Each Order also had a specialty in
their charitable works. For example, the Benedictines focused, not only on
learning in grades K-12, but also on learning at the college and university
level. Thus, education was the forte of the branch of the Sisters of the Order
of St. Benedict at St. Scholastica Academy in Canon City, Colorado.

At this boarding school, 120 young girls filled grades nine-to-
twelve.... The story which follows may provide a "glimpse" of
the enlightening interaction among the nuns and girls.

Black and White and Grape All Over

During the year prior to their graduation in June of 1962, the senior
class members of St. Scholastica Academy were involved in a number of
excursions away from the beautiful, old, residential campus in Canon
City, Colorado. There were trips to visit and celebrate holidays with
orphan children in Pueblo. There were exclusive dress-up dances with
the freshmen at the Air Force Academy in Colorado Springs. There
were trips to view the Royal Gorge with its high suspension bridge, and
the train running on cantilevered tracks at the bottom of the Arkansas

River Canyon. And, there were the unusual trips through the Colorado State Penitentiary to see the "negative elements" of society, and to view the infamous gas chamber. An aside: The location of the Penitentiary was often referred to as the "West Canon Hotel," the Academy as the "Middle Canon Hotel," and the Abbey, the boys' boarding school, as the "East Canon Hotel."

The interest in such trips was superseded by outdoor, nature excursions. A morning hike, led by the well- endowed Sister Aurelia, had many young ladies gasping for air as they trudged up the high Skyline Drive for an expansive overview of the valley in which Canon City was located. A venture up to the sandstone rocks of Red Canyon gave rise to upbeat versions of songs, such as "Do your boobs hang low? Do they wobble to and fro?…" The dismayed Benedictine nuns who followed the campus truck, cum girls, had no control over the "ladies" boisterous renditions.

However, the favorite adventure away from campus was the spring jaunt to the nearby tree-covered slopes leading to the Wet Mountain Valley. The hike required stamina and skill in negotiating the trails, and crossing Grape Creek. Now, Grape Creek did not have the roaring, churning rapids of the dangerous Arkansas River into which Grape Creek eventually flowed. But, in May, the Creek water was deceptively swift, ankle-to-calf deep, and swept over many of the moss-covered rocks on which each hiker stepped in order to cross to the far bank to then proceed to a delightful, aspen-shaded, grassy, picnic area.

The clear mountain air, the simple beauty of the trees, grass, creek, and, of course, picnic fixings brought out high spirits in each girl. One, there were no classes to attend. Two, there were fewer chances to receive demerits for untoward behavior. And, three, there were no uniforms to wear. Attire for the day-trip consisted of baggy shirts, discreet cut-offs (more like capri-style pants), and tennis shoes. Back at school, firmly shut up in closets, were navy- blue A-line skirts, navy-blue blazers with the school's crest-on-the-breast, white—extremely white—short-sleeve, cotton blouses, and the abhorred black-and-white saddle shoes.

Four nuns of the Order of St. Benedict—Sisters Agnes, Audrey, Aurelia, and Fabian—accompanied the young ladies. These chaperones were also attired in garb befitting the occasion—black shoes, black tunic, black belt, black scapular, black veil, white wimple, and white coif. All outfits were a little more well-worn than their usual daily clothing for teaching. The fact that the Vatican II Council had yet to be held explains why the women were wearing full habits. Of the four prefects, the one who held most authority was Sister Fabian. This fine stately woman was the principal, the head-honcho, the power-wielder of St. Scholastica Academy. Being in her "good graces" was part of being a good student. Certainly there was respect and a bit of awe for her. There was also an outright "What will she do to me if I... ?" sort of apprehension.

The day of said hike found students and faculty in marvelously beneficent moods. Chatter and humor came easily. Even the threesome of "Mac," "V," and "Cec"—noted for their nefarious activities—were kindly accompanying the above-described, stern principal. Then, they came to the crossing of Grape Creek. Most of the girls splashed through the waters keeping some sort of steady footing on the rocks as they tried to negotiate the swirling waters. However, the three girls, being in most generous of spirit, turned to their compadre, Sister Fabian, and offered to help her get across the waters of Grape Creek. They knew that even for a woman of such stature, there would be no Red Sea-parting-of-the-waters to get Sister Fabian to the distant shore. And so, with the brilliance of boarding school minds, Mac, V, and Cec persuaded Sister Fabian that they could carry her across the Creek. They reasoned that the good Sister should not get her shoes and her ankle-length habit wet. Why this devout nun succumbed to the helpful enjoinders of the threesome remains a mystery to this day. Speculation on Wall Street never matched that surrounding what became "The Grape Creek Incident."

Cec and Mac wanted to crisscross, and hook arms and hands to fashion a "chair" upon which Sister Fabian would sit and be transported. They did so. Sister Fabian did sit on the "chair." And, off they went. V led Mac and Cec, cum nun in arms, onto the near shore. Skillfully, she planted each foot on each rock in the Creek, telling Mac and Cec which ones to step on as they held the nun in their arms and began the "crossing of the mighty river," which did sort of remind one of lumbering covered wagons pulled by oxen stumbling into the breach. And stumble they did—the girls and the nun— only a third of their way into the muddy spring waters. With the stumble, "it" all fell apart. The idea, the arms, the "chair," and the nun landed in the icy ripples of Grape Creek. A scream—nobody knows from where—sounded. Then, as if in slow motion, the girls who had crossed the Creek, and the ones preparing to cross, turned with one huge intake of air, and gasped at what literally lay before them—the vision of an imposing, stately nun sitting in a not-so-stately, spread-eagle way amidst the gurgling waters.

While the other girls and nuns froze, Mac, V, and Cec sort of put themselves together to try to pick up Sister Fabian from the Creek. However, she brushed off their muddy ministrations, stood up, and with the soggy habit, trudged the rest of the way across the water. Mac, V, and Cec stood absolutely still, frigid water encircling their legs. Finally, with much effort, they, too, made the other bank, and remained some distance from the saturated nun.

They knew they were doomed. If heavenly bolts of lightning did not strike the threesome, then years and years of polishing silverware, and digging dandelions loomed in their vision of a future of punishments. In each mind ran the question: In the "Rule of St. Benedict," what is the appropriate punishment for nun-dumping? As the three teeth-chattering girls stood contemplating their fate, Sister Fabian slipped off her shoes to pour Grape Creek water from them, and began to wring the cold water from the heavy, now really heavy, soaked fabric of her habit—the black robe and scapular, the white coif and wimple.

Undaunted, and with the grace befitting her role as a guide and model for young women, Sister Fabian grabbed up the hem of her soiled garments and called out, "C'mon girls, Let's move it. We're having a picnic!" Then, the imposing figure strode across the squishy grass to the equally imposing aspen trees. Normally, one refers to those trees as quaking-aspen. However, that day, the ones doing the quaking were the terror-stricken, tragic, trio.

One may ask what did happen to Mac, V, and Cec. For them, punishment was meted out in only warm-hearted smiles, outrageous laughter, and gracious love. Perhaps though, Sister Fabian knew that each of the trio's personal feelings of guilt would be their ever-so-subtle "sentence" of the day, the week, the rest of the year. Cec begged to help the sisters who did all the cooking for the early morning breakfasts. V wanted to run the dishwashing machine after each evening meal, thus missing part of the recreation hour. Mac insisted on polishing all of the knives and forks and spoons until glistening was the operative word. Guilt did serve its purpose for having dunked a nun.

For Cec and her two cohorts, the special glimpse of Black and White and Grape All Over had been indelibly impressed in their thoughts and in their memories.

Miracles can happen. In the following story, a modern miracle occurs
with a vision of a ski trip. The unusual adventure for the young women,
reluctantly granted by their school authorities, provides more miracles
and visions in an aura of white. They see snow. They see Svenn and
more snow. They see little children and lots and lots of snow. And, as
if in a holy vision, they see black and white in new- fallen snow.

Humility, Girls!... Humility!

"Holy Mary, Mother of God! Will you guys be quiet!" It is 1962. It is
a senior sneak trip. Planned by twenty-seven St. Scholastica Academy
boarding school girls, the venture is to provide skiing pleasure at Steamboat
Springs, Colorado. The admonition by the class president, unfortunately,
does little to provide a silent departure by private bus at 4:00 a.m. on a
cold February morning. Two black and white habit-ed Benedictine nuns
accompany the young "women." Despite nun-like censure by Sister Fabian
and Sister Agnes, the song, "Do your boobs hang low? Do they wobble to
and fro? Can you tie them in a knot? Can you tie them in a bow?..." rings
out in bawdy fashion. Similar "indelicate" songs occupy the tedious hours
of the trip from Canon City. The nuns must simply give up.

In Steamboat Springs, the gracious greeting by the owner and staff
noting, "We'd like to welcome all of you to our old, historic hotel." is barely
heard over the excited unloading of the bus and unpacking of ski clothes
and equipment. "Thank you! Glad to be here!" echoes in the lobby as the
group leaves the hotel to excitedly tromp through hip-deep snow paths

to the slopes. The two ever-so-present nuns follow. "Girls… Girls! For goodness sake, slow down!" Their directive goes unheeded.

The young women, cum observant nuns, manage to safely arrive near the lodge for skiing instructions. The two nuns cough disapprovingly of the "oohs" and "aahs" from the young ladies when they first catch sight of their ski instructor. "Mein Gott!" the stunning, handsome Scandinavian utters. "You mean, none uff you ladies haf never put der foot to der ski?" Following his directions, the eager students "put feet to skis." Then, taking a deep breath, Svenn calls, "Fall down…. You must all fall down!" A chorus of "What?" Then, "Why?" meets the frosty air. Svenn does not seem quite as handsome as he did moments before. "Mein dear ladies… you must fall down to learn to get up!" Mumbling. Grumbling. A few "Ahems" from the overseers and all obediently fall down. Svenn smiles indulgently. "Now, you vill stand up… like dis." A scramble of skis and poles ensues with no skier-to-be quite accomplishing directions. The nuns turn to one another with sneaky grins. The minutes of orders from Svenn for "der ladies" turn into what seem like hours of falling down, standing up, ascending the modest hill with criss-cross steps, falling down, standing up, descending the modest hill with cross-ski-braking, falling down, and standing up. The procedure is repeated and repeated and repeated.

At the first day's end, the now not-so-stalwart seniors hobble with Neanderthal bent-knee gait to dine with the overly cheery Benedictines. The "ladies" chit-chat, but merriment is somewhat subdued during dinner. It appears aches and pains of exertion have overcome them. Sleep comes quickly that evening.

At early morning's light, the seniors who now consider themselves hardy athletes huff-puff icy breaths on their way up the slopes to meet with their favorite Svenn. "You vill use der rope-tow to go up der hill today.... Den, you vill come down." How they "vill come down" is not explained. Sister Fabian and Sister Agnes, the ever-present chaperones, laugh quietly.

A few beginners master use of the rope-tow, as they straighten their skis, grab the leather strap, and glide upward to the landing, triumphant in their skill.... "We made it! Look, guys, we made it!" Most of the beginners, however, inadvertently hook an elbow in the strap, lose footing, and are dragged through the snow to the landing, not-so- triumphant in their skill. Little five and six-year-old skiers skillfully schuss up to the bedraggled girls, and add a bit of insult. "Hey, look! You made it up the Bunny Hill!" Svenn has not told the neophytes the name of the beginners' hill. When one embarrassed senior threatens them with her ski poles, the laughing, giggling, urchins zip off with Olympian skill.

Now the moment arrives. Once up the slope, the would-be-skiers must go down. As the young ladies gather for their next challenge, they catch sight of one daring senior extricating herself from the rope-tow, at the next level. Before they cheer her endeavors, they see the Ski Patrol strap her into a rescue basket to begin the usual head-first descent down the mountain. When they then fear that a cohort has been injured, they hear a loud and firm, "Stop!" The progress of the Patrol halts. Cecilia, one of the more adventurous souls, wants the Patrol to reverse the basket so she will have an exciting view of her journey down the slope. There is some relief, coupled with a bit of jealousy, when they realize Cec has used the ruse of injury and found the best way to get back to the toasty warm lodge unscathed.

After that interruption, the other twenty-six, anxiety-ridden, would-be-skiers face the prospect of six-foot-deep snow. Desire to exit the Bunny Hill conquers the terror. Each sort of "schusses" down the hill. And, each finds herself buried in a huge drift with arms, legs, skis, and poles askew. They mutter. They sputter. They shout defiantly, "I'm just gonna stay in this freakin' snow all day long!" Each, in turn hears the twin voices of Sister Fabian and Sister Agnes rising like a Gregorian chant, "Humility, girls! Remember Humility!"

Three days of "Bunny-sloping" provide an emotional high for each senior, even though the days provide only a modicum of physical prowess. The waning sunlight brings a final day's closing to the "sneak" trip. Except... except for one final ski-slope activity. The smiling nun-ly duo comes from their "watching post" in the warm lodge only to be met by seniors holding two sets of boots and poles and skis. "OK, Sisters.... It's *your* turn!" "Really, girls. Good gracious! We can't... we won't!" But, there they stand, just as Svenn appears in time to urge off their shoes, put on boots, strap on skis, and hand over poles. The process happens quickly. There is no more time for protests. A camera- toting crowd gathers around the students and the nuns. The latter in their black-and-white flowing religious habits resemble, truly resemble, Emperor penguins... on skis! A cheer grows: "Ski... Ski... Ski!" Both nuns stand aghast at their dilemma. And... promptly fall down, with skis and poles pointing in all directions of a compass.

Silence.... The nuns are silent.... The onlookers are silent.... The students are silent. But then... rising to the heavens like a Gregorian chant, the seniors begin: "Humility, Sisters! Remember, Humility!"

Although the highlight, the fitting conclusion to the trip seems to be the admonition for "Humility," another occurrence marks the sneak trip as classic in the annals of senior activities beyond 1962. Once all the women return to the old hotel, they are treated to a fine dinner of corn chowder, tossed garden salad, smoothly mashed potatoes, rich brown gravy, and perfectly prepared beef medallions. Dessert offers two large scoops of homemade vanilla ice cream atop a large chocolate-chip cookie, all drizzled with caramel sauce, whipped cream, and a bright maraschino cherry.

The leader of the Academy troops, has the hotel staff assemble for her Thank-You speech and cheers from the twenty-seven seniors. The planned early bus departure and all the food has meant an early trip to bed and lights out. All is calm until, at 2:00 a.m., the sound of ever more frequent flushing of toilets begins. Two hardy nuns and twenty-some girls spend the rest of the night with a major intestinal disturbance. Fear of food poisoning prompts an ill Sister Fabian to check the girls in each room. No food item is the culprit. The night finally comes to an end, but not the dilemma.

With misery abounding, somehow the bus does get loaded with baggage and moaning, groaning sick seniors. A kind, old, gentlemanly doctor, contacted by the hotel staff, assesses the situation, and... laughs. The attack of diarrhea, and its accompanying difficulties, has been caused by the area's sulfur water which all the students and nuns had copiously consumed. Following the chuckling physician's sage advice, Sister Fabian purchases a case of Kaopectate to be taken to relieve the incapacitating symptoms.

Once the return trip is underway, the chalky-elixir is distributed tablespoon by tablespoon, over and over, to each sick person by the stalwart, tablespoon thief, Cec. The bus driver, also afflicted, simply drinks his doses from his own bottle. However, in his kindness and for his own good, he stops the bus at every little berg on the route, so he and the girls can run to any nearby restroom. The surge of bodies looks like a herd of wild horses escaping corral confinement.

By the time the entourage passes through Colorado Springs, many difficult hours later, the moaning, and consumption of Kaopectate has almost ceased. The students and the nuns probably never have felt such relief to see the grounds of the Academy. The mantra now is: Home is where the beds, and the empty toilet stalls, are.

The story does not quite end with such relief. Word of the seniors' skiing adventure and safe return reaches every freshman, sophomore, junior, and, of course, every nun. The unexpected distress that occurred was to be an unstated, secret, part of the story of the trip. At assembly the next afternoon, the junior-class president welcomes home the seniors, and congratulates them on their "sneaky trip." After a dramatic pause, she spills the unspeakable secret. With relish, the junior cleverly details the illness portion of the seniors' and nuns' adventure. She notes the cost of the trip—for the case of Kaopectate, and the relief sought at every little gas station. With solemnity, she pronounces that the senior class of 1962, will be forever and for all time addressed as "The Kaopectate Kids." And, she further pronounces that the two valiant and resolute nuns, Sister Fabian and Sister Agnes, will be forever and for all time remembered as the "Shining Skiing Sisters."

There is another dramatic pause. Then, the assembled non-skiers, the left-behind-ones, the freshmen, the sophomores, the juniors, stand to give a hearty, boisterous, Academy cheer to the seniors and to the nuns:

"Humility, Ladies!… Remember, Humility!"

Dear Cec...

On August 9, 2014, you—Cecilia McNulty Woods—left this life as we know it. You died to become an essence of peace and love, to nurture in a beautiful way all those beings you met and knew for nearly seventy-one years. In your special being now, I know you will still share your joy, your laughter, your exhilaration.

Do recall, Cec, that in all you did in this place, you chose to say that your glass was always half-full. And, you more than hinted, in your inimitable way, that I, too frequently, saw my glass as half-empty. Cec, you must know that at times I didn't even have a doggone glass.

Actually, my dear friend, you lived with your glass totally filled—with love. That love is your gift—a gift to all of us. It is a gift to hold close—forever.

OTHER CONSIDERATIONS

What is hoped for and prayed for by a child can become
extraordinary, can become miraculous.

I Am Maria.

"Please, Holy Santa Maria, help me....Please, protect my family....
Please, we go far away. I do not know what will happen to us....Please,
Santa Maria...." the young girl whispered the appeal.

"Come on.... Hurry up!" The man in gray uniform shout. Our little family hold together as we move in line. Sign say, *"Declaracion de Aduanas."* I think it mean "customs." I am not so sure what "customs" mean. I am afraid of big place, and noise, and so many people.

Papa Pedro, Mama Consuela, little brother Jesus come to big United States. I am Maria. I am ten.

"Passport?" The man in gray suit ask. Papa confused.

"Pasaporte, Papa! The man he want to see Passport." Papa stand proud and give man little book. Papa speak clearly. *"Pasaporte Numero*: 9-2-6-3-5-6-2-7-9." He work for many days to remember numbers. "Country of Issue?" the man ask. *"Pais que lo expide,* Papa." "Ah, Mexico," he answer.

I not understand why gray man ask Papa this question. Gold stamp of Mexico is on Passport. I think man does not like us. "Where are you going?" This time I answer for Papa. "Colorado."

"Yeah, but where in Colorado?" The man glare. "To the San Luis Valley. We go to pick potatoes."

"I didn't ask you that!" the man snap at me. "Now, Miss Smarty Pants, if you know so much, whose farm are you going to?"

I do not know "Miss Smarty Pants." But, I say, "We go to Mister Harold Rogers' farm. He need us there."

"Where you gonna live, little girl?" He raise his voice. He smile. It is not good smile. I do not like gray man's questions.

"We stay with relatives—family of Isaac Manzanares on farm. We go there in our pickup." "We go there in our pickup…" the man repeat with sneer. "Your bags. Let me see them!"

Papa look at me. I point to put our sacks of clothes and old brown suitcase on table. The gray man open them. "Nothing much here…. Guess you're OK." He stamp Passport. We stand still. "Well, what're you waitin' for… a limousine? Get your stuff and go….*Vamos!*"

Papa start to get mad. "No, Papa!" I grab his hand so we can all hurry to pickup. Me and Jesus climb in back to sit with bags and suitcase. We go almost all day long. Is not short trip to Mister Rogers' place, I think.

Is dark, now. Papa drive all night through little towns in New Mexico. Me and Jesus snuggle deep down among bags to keep warm. He is frightened, so I hold him close so he fall asleep. When sun come over mountains, Papa stop pickup in town called "Antonito." I think this town is good. St. Anthony help all people.

"Welcome to Colorado, How're ya all doin'?" a friendly man ask. Papa smile. It is first time I see Papa smile in many, many days. We all smile. I ask man how to get to "Monte Vista" and find "Mister Rogers."

"Well, go north to Alamosa—you know, to the Cottonwoods by the big river, the Rio Grande. Then go west to the town with a view of mountains— Monte Vista. Ask for Mr. Rogers at the filling station with the red star."

"Don't go to sleep, Jesus. Look at beautiful mountains—Sangre de Christos. They are Blood of Christ!" Then, Papa drive north to big town of Alamosa… at least it seem big. It not like our little adobe village in Mexico. I call to Papa. "Go left, go left," when we reach crossroads. There are many, many cottonwood trees, all yellow in fall color.

Papa now drive west toward mountains. Along road are chico bushes and sagebrush like in Mexico. Then… "Look, Jesus! Look, Mama! Look, Papa!" We see fields and fields of potatoes. We see big tractors and trucks. I never see so many before. It take my breath away! Finally, we come to town of Monte Vista. Everything is all bright and shiny.

"Look, look at trucks and cars!" Jesus yell real loud. "Sh—sh—sh—be quiet! They will not like us."

Papa find filling station with red star. "Texaco," it say. Man at station grin. "You've come to pick 'taters, I bet…. Who you lookin' for?" Papa look at me. "Mister Harold Rogers," I say. "Oh, yeah. Well, go south here and then go west at the Lariat Road." Man tell me letters…"L-A-R-I-A-T."

Papa follow my directions. We go by grassy fields with many, many white sheep, then lots and lots of potato fields. We stop at sign by big gate to small lane. "This is Mister Rogers' farm!" We see house close by and people come running, waving to us. "Papa! Mama! Is Uncle Isaac and everybody!" We are happy. They are happy. We hug and kiss. We laugh. We are finally together as big family.

A dusty red pickup come down the little road to us. Everybody get quiet. It stop and man—tall like Papa—get out. "Isaac?" "Hey, Mister Harold, come meet my family!" Man smile when Uncle Isaac wave for us to come to him. I like his smile. I think I like this man! Mr. Rogers—Mister

Harold— give Papa a strong handshake, also Jesus. He tip his hat and gently take Mama's hand, and then my hand.

"It's very nice to meet your family, Isaac. I'm glad they made it here. I brought a few gifts for you. Oranges and apples for the little ones—and some tasty lamb to cook. Enjoy the sunny afternoon! I'll see you all in the morning."

Me and Jesus very tired, but all us kids still play hide-and-seek in the grass, the trees, and bushes. Isaac's Grandma Rosa make wonderful lamb stew for supper. She fix it with red potatoes, bright carrots, and yellow onions. And bunch of green chilis and spices! Finally, everybody fall asleep on soft mattresses and warm blankets from Mister Harold.

It much too early when Uncle Isaac call to come to breakfast of beans, tortillas, and coffee. We eat and then he take us to potato fields. Mister Harold already is on tractor with machine digging potatoes that come out on top of dirt. The sun is coming up when Uncle Isaac give us baskets for potatoes to pick up. Work is hard. We carry heavy loads—basket after basket—to large "sorter." There Aunt Estella throw out rocks and vines. Little and big potatoes go on different chains into what she call "burlap bags." Papa and Cousin Tomas quickly sew closed each bag with sharp needles and long white strings. Then men—my cousins Francisco, Juan, Pablo, Estafan—load trucks with potato bags to take to white-painted adobe storage buildings. All goes very fast. Aunt Dolo and Aunt Lucia help us and hurry us kids along ahead of the sorter.

It is hot by noon. We stop under trees to rest and eat Grandma Rosa's, oh so good, lamb sandwiches. Then we go to pick more potatoes until sun go down. Mister Harold come to us kids. "You're doing a great job, so I'm going to pay you fifty cents for each row you pick." There is lots of potato rows. I never seen so much money before. Jesus and me give money to Mama to keep for our family.

We barely eat supper before me, Jesus, and cousins fall asleep. Morning come too soon each day. All of us work very hard, but also tell stories and jokes. Uncle Isaac keep us moving and remind us of money we can make. "Come on. Work a little faster." For many days and days, we pick potatoes. True to his word, Mister Harold pay us money each day. He trust Uncle Isaac and Papa and all of us that we will not go away early before all potatoes are picked.

Then it happen.... Near end of harvest, Mister Harold tell Uncle Isaac, Papa, Mama, Jesus, and me to come to his "office." He call nobody else to this place. Me—all of us—so afraid we have done something wrong. But, Mister Harold tell Papa—with Uncle Isaac's help—that he like our little family. He want us not to go back to Mexico. He want all of us to stay, to live with him on his big farm. He say, "You've all worked so hard. You've showed me you are good people. I am very pleased with your family,... So, if you want I'll start to help you stay in this country." Our little family very quiet. We do not know what to do.

Mister Harold go on. He say he want Papa to help care for big herds of sheep. He want Mama to cook and clean in his house. He look at me and Jesus. "And you two will need to go to school." I cannot believe what Mister Harold say! He must like us very much! Papa and Mama will have work. Me and Jesus will learn many things. It is true. We will not have to go back to Mexico. We will all live in big United States. There is only one thing left now to do:

"Dear Holy Santa Maria, I no more doubt your care
and love. You have brought us many good things. You have
brought us to good place. I have prayed to you, Santa Maria.
You have answered my prayers. Gracias.... Gracias....
I am Maria. I am ten.

What can be seen in these words is a story—one with Thoughts, Hopes, Dreams, and possible Reality.

Fade to Black

The house lights dimmed slowly. Quiet settled over the filled seats of the well-appointed theatre. There was the obligatory cough or two as patrons awaited the moment when the "grand rag" would gracefully, silently rise. Then came the magic—the transformation from practical affairs of the day to a willing suspension of disbelief. An evening of theatre had begun.

As if in another world, she waited to enter the first scene. With purpose, she would cross through a sand-colored, old adobe-like arch, Spanish in structure. Her intense black, high-necked, floor-length dress bespoke aged authority. The lustrous black lace mantilla covering her silver-gray hair provided her a regal bearing. She would pause, and give a gracious nod of acknowledgement to those who honored her as the elder she was, now accompanying her son to his marriage. The look, the wave of her hand, and the reassuring pat on the arm of her tall, black-haired beloved spoke volumes to the hushed, anticipating audience. For them, the story was just beginning.

The old woman, actually a young actor, also felt anticipation, a pensive, melancholy sort of anticipation. This night was to be an ending. Her visions were culminating in her final performance as "The Mother" in the play "Blood Wedding." This high poetic tragedy by Federico Garcia Lorca had captivated her for months. Even the sound of the noted dramatist's name held a touching enchantment. The storied poem of love, anger, jealousy, rage, and loss became hers, she imagined, the evening of auditions. She knew she was "The Mother"—the old Spanish matriarch— as she left the theatre that brisk, winter night. "Read-throughs" with the new script in hand brought to her a subdued sense of hesitancy and anxiety. Was it a fear of not being good enough? Would she be able to meet the demands of her new role? She shivered, not from the cold, but from the thoughts and doubts she tried to stop.

She smiled for a moment in fanciful reminiscence. Silently, secretly, she chuckled in recalling her role in "You Can't Take It With You." What on earth had she, as the "Grand Duchess Olga Katrina," really known about blintzes? Had she really kissed the crazy imposter in "Thieves' Carnival?" She thought he may have been the most handsome of actors when they tried to negotiate the intricate dance steps of the tango. And, how could she not help re-imagining her role as "Ma Allen" in "Dark of the Moon." Did she dare think of her delightful, Appalachian- dialect, vocal debut with "A pur gal lef' her muther... !" Again, she laughed quietly, privately.

Then, the concealed reminiscence turned to sadness when, as "Lady Alice More," she had last touched the hand of her beloved "Sir Thomas." Deep inside, she had experienced, had identified with the doomed conclusion in "A Man For All Seasons." Memory begot memory and hidden tears. There had been no applause from the stunned audience when "Otto Frank" spoke the final lines in "Diary of Anne Frank." She wondered about the unique theatre-in-the-square production. Had she fully interpreted the persevering character of "Mrs. Frank?" Or were her thoughts now just a shrouded token of an imaginary moment?

Though young in years, she imagined herself frequently cast as an older woman. Directors would tell her she had a "mature" quality to her voice, that she "aged well" in stage make-up. She smiled with positive reflections of her dreams.

These recollections passed by, flowed quickly now as she turned to the theatrical reality when the lighting instruments would focus on the "Blood Wedding" entrance to come. Her achievement on the snowy evening of auditions meant learning line after line of script. And, not only memorizing them comma by comma, but also interpreting them as the director wished. She imagined an inner thrill of adeptness at blocking—knowing exactly when and how to turn, where to be for each movement in a scene. Easily she summoned a command of stage directions, and smiled knowingly when told to "cross to down-stage-left." That meant she would have the strongest position on the stage from which to deliver her lines. Thinking that she would deliver her final speech in Lorca's drama at "DSL" gave her an adrenaline rush.

Bit-by-bit, as rehearsals progressed, the old "materfamilias" took form, both on-stage and off-stage. She dreamed that Stanislavski would be so proud of her. She visualized a special camaraderie among the members of the large company. Some cast members, such as the groom, the bride-to-be, the ex-lover, the bride's father, a few assorted aunts and uncles were those she would have liked as her real-world family. The quirky, gentle lady, who ran the broken-down restaurant near the theatre, teased them as night after night following rehearsals she served each of them two huge, greasy, crispy chicken drumsticks and ketchup-slathered fries. Warm laughter and mutual care could make the weeks of rehearsals less daunting.

Culmination of the days of her work was to be attained on opening night of "Blood Wedding." As she hoped, the actors' and technicians' "Break-a-Leg" encouragements filled the backstage hallways and dressing rooms. Before her first acting performance, she recalled having a hand clasped over her mouth when, as a neophyte to tradition, she almost uttered the bad-luck call of "Good Luck, Everyone!" There also had been the frozen seconds when she realized: "My god, there are people out there in those seats!" At that instant, her acting cohort had grabbed her arm and quickly rushed her onstage for a memorable squabbling scene.

Sometimes anxiety about her acting ventures found calming compensation when she visualized, when she dreamed of assurance in her art. New-found wit would pepper her conduct in rehearsals. She anticipated phones ringing unexpectedly as they had for the great Barrymores, of set furniture and pieces placed slightly askew, and of being thrown an off beat, incongruent line. She saw herself recovering from any mishap with remarkable agility.

Then, as she had imagined, this evening's production began. All reverie ceased as she once again embraced her character of the strong-willed "Mother," and crossed from the stage-left-wing to the arch at center-stage. Memory would serve her well as it had in play after play, production after production. There had been entrances, exits, and applause—warm, energizing, enfolding. Onstage, she felt accepted for her art and for the feelings deep inside her. Offstage, she too often knew doubt and heaviness within herself.

The closing performance of the production of "Blood Wedding" would bring to her a personal ending as well as the conclusion of Lorca's tragedy. She gathered strength for the final moments. She felt the solo instrument focus white light on that down-stage-left position for the last time. Power of recall gave life to her words, to her actions. "The Mother" sank slowly to her knees. In a speech to her murdered son, the old woman wailed about a knife, about a stabbing, about a lifeless body—about a deep, dark, paralyzing scream. "The Mother's" words were to be her final words. All became dark. Slowly the heavy curtain came down, and the house lights came up.

Then came the words of another mother: "Hey, you little bitch! The stupid kid's yellin' an' cryin' again. Now, get in there an' take care of it... or I'll take care of you. You hear me? An' get yourself into this kitchen an' fix the damn supper. That is... if you ain't off dreamin' theatre again!"

Fade to black.

Silent self-conversations, seen and heard in our mind, often typify what we
wish we could say, or would have said, to someone, articulating our inner
dialogue as precisely as we desire. We long to have had the opportunity to
speak directly, even forcefully, to one for whom we cared deeply, for whom
we held long, abiding love, for whom we held our tongue and closed our eyes
to myriad, wayward, indiscretions. That someone now is gone, and only
in our mind can we speak to ourselves the words. Perhaps, one person did
have her conversation of thoughts, of perceptions, of feelings. She spoke to one
who was dear to her, but also to one who had brought her much emotional
pain. She spoke to one whose actions made her challenge herself to go beyond
mere duty to him. She had her conversation, imagined though it was, with
him at the last…. Franklin was dead, and she, Eleanor, spoke to him.

Unspoken Thoughts

"I can permit myself only unspoken thoughts, Franklin. Silence now remains our last bond. You and I share this time, this place; yet, we are separated as so often we have been. This is your last journey—you in repose in the train car draped in black. I, also in black, sit in my stiff seat noting person after person standing by the tracks in final obeisance to you. Arms extended, eyes daubed by kerchiefs, hats placed over hearts. It is not for the usual presence of your warm, endearing smile, nor for your infectious joy, that your presidential train slows its pace on a journey carrying us to that marbled city we have known as home.

The tilt of your head, jaw jutting forward, long cigarette holder firmly raised as in victory—you knew what you were doing, Franklin. You were exuding images, not of fear, but of hope, of possibility, of greatness. When you spoke, your people, indeed the world, listened and clung to each word of care, love, anger, and defiance. Your persona grabbed the senses. You gave hope in a time when life did not seem possible.

And so, there you were, Franklin—beloved as a president, as a man. But, my dear, you were a person of two lives. Your dynamism and vitality seemed to run on two separate tracks. You must know how your public behavior contrasted with your private activities, hidden and closed to the world, known only to the few. I was one of those few. My reserve prevented me from open, public confrontation. I had not yet acquired skill for the attack, Franklin. Although, I did imagine conversations then in which I would berate your unfaithfulness, your absence of loyalty to me. I, perhaps, accepted your actions because I doubted myself in matters of such intimacy. Ever so early, we began to define our relationship. Mental acuity was our forte, our strength, Franklin. We did learn to engage our minds for singularly notable accomplishments, albeit that I came late to our endeavors.

What held us together, Franklin, for so many long years? Your dear mother certainly played a questionable role in our relationship. Remember? She never quite approved of our joining. You never challenged her wedding gift of our New York townhouse, even as she resided with us displaying her control and power in our lives. I accept that I offered you no glamour. Rather plain-of-face, long-necked, gawky, I did offer you my mind—as you did offer yours to me. We were, indeed, sexually intimate for a time. Your almost insatiable appetite brought us our six children. Then, our early intimacy waned. No doubt, those children will tell our story many years hence. Recall that the press corps has always been discreet regarding most of your private life.

Oh, Franklin, what occurred in our life separated us in trust—my trust in you, my trust in myself. You cannot help but to remember those times, those early events. She was *my* social secretary, Franklin. And, you... you took her as far more than a frivolous dalliance. The association was one of intimacy. You and Miss Mercer—you and my Lucy—shared beyond mere kindly friendship. In the favor I was doing to unpack your suitcase from that London trip, I discovered your letters of love to her, Franklin. Oh, what a field-day your admiring press would have had with that more than a hint of sexual scandal. I wanted to depart, to leave you. But, a disgraceful divorce seemed never meant for us. The threat of losing a burgeoning political career, the threat of losing generous financial resources from your mother, the threat of losing an intellectual companionship brought you to realize you had to reject Lucy.

My dear, I believe we developed a melancholy type of lonely hearts relationship. Yet, in time, I became less shy, less reserved, less weak. I became your voice on many occasions when evidence of your paralysis threatened your successes. But, what did you do, Franklin? You distantly, quietly, remained loyal to that woman—that Lucy— throughout all your years.

What other women figured so closely in your life? Do you think that I did not know of them? Oh, the glamorous, young Princess Martha of Norway certainly held more than a passing interest, didn't she? Why such need? Your tall, slim, grey-eyed, private secretary also served you— as mistress—for twenty years. Of course, I knew of *her* —your Missy LeHand. I do not believe you ever knew I approved of that relationship, Franklin. Why else would I have allowed you and Missy to work, to occupy, to share adjoining bedrooms?

Why? Why, Franklin, could you not be satisfied? Did you talk to others of your loves? With your loyal cronies? With that Missouri haberdasher Truman? With the foreign greats? Did Winston chuckle knowingly as you whispered of your interests? Did your staunch generals share of their own weak affairs? You even risked exposure of your affair with Miss LeHand, when you took your presidential train to visit her. I do wonder why I was even a bit sad for you when a stroke took her from you. For in your loneliness that followed, my dear, you turned once again to that other woman—your favored Lucy. It pains me so much to recall discovering, on that horrible wind-blown day in September, that you had a most serious, ongoing, affair with the beautiful, sophisticated Lucy. How, oh how, could I have continued still to protect you, to accept what no right-minded woman would ever accept.

What did you and she have, Franklin? What did she offer you? If you were to stand before the members of your cabinet, the members of Congress, the members of your adoring press, what would you say about your relationships, your princess, your Missy, your Lucy, your sins? Do you think I would consider standing with you? What a thought- provoking self-examination I would undergo. That personal act, however, would not take much time. Yes, Franklin, I *would* stand by you, because… well, because. You do know why, don't you? Can you not recall that we have sought, that we have fought for so much of the same good for the world?

However, I must admit my doubts, my fears, my pains have been re-awakened during these past, dark, days. I have come to you in your death, Franklin. But, when that god-awful cerebral hemorrhage struck you, who was with you? Who held your hand? Who, though you were not yet gone, ran to another cottage at our lovely Warm Springs home? Yes, Franklin, your beloved Lucy ran—away from you, away from me, and away from the assembling press. Yes, I admit to feelings of jealousy. But, they were there just for a time, Franklin.

I have been with you in your death. I remain with you—alone. Well, not quite alone. Your people out there claim you, also. They do not know of what they will, in later years, judge as sexual scandal. But, I have known, Franklin.

Now, I must come, will come into my own life. As I recount our time together, I will not be held forever in mourning. I will move forward. I will achieve.

Franklin, somehow through all our days, we still had a good dependence, a good respect, a good mutual admiration. Somehow, we did.... It is late now. It is dark now. Night has fallen, as we must all fall. I shall remember you always, my dear.... I have loved.... I have loved you, Franklin."

"I am especially grateful to Dr. Ray E. Wagner, who not only graciously served as chairman of my doctoral committee, but also provided unbounded support, inspiration, and insight mingled with warm, gentle humor and understanding. He is, indeed, a gentle- man, a mentor, and a friend. It is to him that this dissertation is dedicated."

Because We Can Love One Another

The phone rang. I reluctantly picked up the receiver. "Hello…"

"Roberts, meet me at the south entrance to your building. I'll be there in ten minutes." "But, Wags, I'm doing…" "Roberts… Just be there!"

I was there. Wags did meet me. I crawled into the passenger seat of his old, blue Nissan. "Where are we going?"

"You'll see soon enough." he responded.

And, soon I did. In a matter of minutes, we pulled into the boat dock of Dow Lake. The Lake, in a valley near Athens, Ohio, frequently saw the likes of sunbathers and swimmers, boaters and rafters. I had been to Dow Lake any number of times, but I had never noticed canoes at the dock. However, there sat one, a reddish-maroon-colored canoe, bobbing in the dark-green water.

"Ray… What are we doing here?" Sometimes I called him "Wags," and sometimes "Ray." The names used by his graduate advisees varied in a happenstance way. However, for truly formal occasions, we addressed him as "Dr. Wagner," according him his due respect.

On that warm, late Fall day, after I donned a bright orange life-vest (He knew I swam like a rock.), we took paddles in hand, and used them to glide that canoe—his canoe—across Dow Lake toward a large grouping of brown and green cattails. I began to inquire again about our destination.

"Sh-sh," he whispered. "You'll see soon enough."

Wags turned the canoe and urged it through a small opening in the reeds. Slowly, we emerged into another part of the Lake, a part seldom seen by most visitors. He guided the canoe along the outer edge of some late-blooming, soft-pink, and yellow water lilies. Only five yards away, duos of Canada geese, attired in identical uniforms of black, brown, and white feathers, moved effortlessly on the mirror-like water. They made no sound. We stilled the canoe. We made no sound. I did almost gasp in wonder when I saw a tall, Great Blue Heron searching for water bugs along some marshy grasses. Nearby, on an exposed, bare, half-sunken, tree branch, an elegant Snowy Egret stolidly stood, observing us, as we observed him.

Those delicate moments of silence were suddenly interrupted by a loud slap, then a second, signaling an alarm that intruders, Ray and I, had violated someone's territory. Ray smiled warmly at me, then, carefully pointed toward a half-submerged beaver den.

In silent awe, there in that canoe, tears filled my eyes. The scenes had so overwhelmed my senses that I hardly noticed Ray moving the canoe out of that inner sanctum back to the gentle ripples of the wide, open Lake. I just sat, rather benumbed, as we slowly headed toward the boat dock.

"I don't know what to say, Ray."

"Don't say anything, yet. Just take time to absorb your small moment of peace."

The experience had, indeed, brought peace. In that almost sacred space, my mind had set aside classes in symbol systems, readings for comprehensive exams, and preparations for a dissertation proposal. "Busyness" had occupied me, had been my nemesis.

When we reached the dock, I extricated myself from the canoe, and crossed the grass to a small, wooden, picnic table. Ray went to the Nissan, and brought over two mugs and a thermos. We sat quietly for a few minutes, sipping the strong, dark-roast coffee.

"Well, Roberts… Let's talk a bit…. It seems like you've chosen a topic for your tome." He smiled, then, grinned in a questioning way. "Just how are you going to join the thoughts of the Father of the Atom Bomb with the thoughts of the Father of Twentieth-Century Rhetoric? That question was the beginning of a 10-month dialogue that guided research, development, writing, presentation, and defense of "A Rhetorical Analysis of the Security Clearance Hearing of J. Robert Oppenheimer Utilizing Selected Concepts of Kenneth Burke."

During that nearly year-long process, Ray brought other "moments of peace," when he sensed that stress was playing too big a part in my life. There were thinking-cogitating moments. There were directive moments. There were delightful, quirky moments. Ray took me for delicious bowls of lentil soup at the Town House Restaurant, where each week we exchanged perspectives on my plans. Ray called me to come to his open, wood-slatted deck where, over 3-4 beers, he made me agree that 476 sources merited the beginning of my writing of "it." Ray entered my T.A. office one frigid, winter day, carrying a huge, triple-dip, vanilla-chocolate-strawberry, ice-cream cone. "Here, Roberts, you need this. It's been a hot time in the old dissertation town, today!"

Just when it seemed that a day was "too much," Ray's deep, rumbling, infectious, laughter would ring out and echo down the corridors of Kantner Hall. One could not help but feel a burden lifting. Not only for me, did Ray provide gentle support, he also gave fully of himself to my graduate student cohorts, and to the loving undergraduates he faithfully taught each term.

Then, finally, the time came. At precisely 11:00 a.m., on April 27, 1984, I entered the formal "Red Room" of Kantner Hall. I knew well the four, fine gentlemen, who stood to "welcome" me to my dissertation defense. They, Dr. Paul Boase, Dr. Gilford Crowell, Dr. Ernest Collins, and Dr. John Timmis, III, were formally introduced by Dr. Wagner. We sat to begin queries and answers about the dissertation. Each had only modest, inquisitive remarks, as my pulse rate and blood pressure began a slow descent. But, then the ancient "flight or fight response" almost took over when Dr. Wagner cleared his throat and said, "There is one concern I have about your work."

At that moment, I knew the proverbial dissertation-axe was to fall, and I stiffened myself for the blow. "Yes, sir?"

"Well, after perusing these 293 pages for the last time, I noticed a major error." There was a ghastly pregnant pause. Then, he continued, "I believe you need a comma after the introductory clause in sentence 13 of page 172."

"I'll have it fixed right away, sir." I quickly asserted.

"You will. I'm sure of that." he said, as he gave me, and then the rest of the committee his impish smile.

I was soon excused from the "defense." I made my way to the lobby, and paced. Five, then, ten minutes, or an eternity it seemed, passed before

Dr. Wagner called me to return into the Red Room. When I entered, the other four professors stood. There were only smiles. Then came that never-to-be-forgotten moment. Dr. Ray Wagner graciously extended his hand to me and grasped mine firmly. "Welcome to the fraternity, Dr. Elizabeth Roberts." Trying to be very adult-like, I held back tears.

I still must hold back tears, when I remember those precious, indelible, moments—when I recall classes in which I felt no fear; when I recall support that made me a University Fellow; when I recall lentil soup, beer, and ice cream cone; and, especially, when I recall soft waters, cattails, geese, heron, egret, and beaver.

After I left Ohio University, Dr. Wagner always seemed to keep me in his thoughts. At the most wonderful, opportune times, there'd be evening phone calls. And, he would chat about his work, his delightful companion and wife Tish, his semi-retirement, his full retirement, his new avocation as a radio program host, and—his brief, cancerous, illness.

"Roberts?"… He had never stopped calling me, "Roberts." "Roberts, I just wanted you to know I'm reviewing memories these days. I'm waiting for the slap of that beaver tail."

On July 14, 2011, Dr. Ray E. Wagner slept his way forever into memories. He had taught us to see that in this vast, immense, boundless world we can love one another.

Ending Thoughts

These glimpses are finished, perhaps. I have shared much of my life in these pages. I found it terribly difficult, even frightening, to put some glimpses into written forms. However, I delightfully enjoyed arranging many other glimpses into their singular shapes.

As I wrote each piece, my vision improved in both literal and figurative ways. There were, though, many times when those pieces written and those in my mind yet to be written had to be placed aside, to be put away. At those times I could not see—literally could not see—because my eyesight was impaired.

In figurative ways, my vision slowly improved, seemingly with a sense of purpose. In my thoughts, I set right many long injured feelings. I gave voice to that which was negative. I also gave voice to the positive feelings— with pleasure and sometimes bittersweet joy. In writing of events from the past and the present, and in writing of relationships forged over many years, I believe my perceptions of life are more clear to me than at any other time.

I hope that you, my reader, might find your own voice and renewed vision should you so desire. Having cast a look at my life, having glimpsed certain times, events, and people, yet knowing so many more, so many other glimpses still remain, may I say—Now I Can See.

www.ingramcontent.com/pod-product-compliance
Lightning Source LLC
Chambersburg PA
CBHW021615120626
46545CB00001B/245